COLLINS REFERENCE

SPEAKING
IN PUBLIC

Louise Bostock
Consultant: Philip Bowry

HarperCollins*Publishers*

HarperCollins Publishers
P.O. Box, Glasgow G4 0NB

First published 1994

Reprint 10 9 8 7 6 5 4 3 2 1 0

© Book Creation Services 1994

ISBN 0 00 470264 6

Printed in China

CONTENTS

INTRODUCTION

Communication is a watchword for our time. Yet few people have ever thought it necessary to learn the art of effective communication through speech. These are the great unheard – millions of people who every day fail to communicate their needs, opinions and ideas to others.

On the other hand, those who have learned how to get their message across effectively, realize that they have more say in every situation they find themselves in, from proposing a toast to arguing against a planning application, from getting a business proposition accepted by the board to negotiating better facilities for the local hospital. Even in one-to-one conversations, the skilled speaker commands attention and respect, making him or her more capable of communicating successfully in the workplace, with family and friends and in local or national politics.

Collins Pocket Reference Speaking in Public shows that speaking in public is a skill that can be learned like any other, rather than a rare talent confined to the lucky few.

The book is divided into two sections. The first deals with the **Practical Techniques** required to research, prepare and deliver a successful speech on any subject. It stresses the importance of thorough preparation and rehearsal and tells you what questions you must take into account if you are to get your message across to your audience. It also gives hints on how to use the English language to its best effect and how to go about creating and presenting visual aids.

Most of us resist speaking up in public because we are frightened of making fools of ourselves. The last part of the section on Practical Techniques shows you how to control your anxiety and put your nerves to work to your advantage.

The second section, **Roles and Events**, covers a large

v

INTRODUCTION

number of situations in which you may be asked to speak, for example, at work, on social and family occasions or at special events. It includes tips on participating in business meetings, giving wedding speeches, making after-dinner speeches, giving lectures and slide shows, speaking impromptu, debating, fund-raising speeches and proposing toasts. It provides details of what to expect on the day and some ideas for content, along with reminders of how to avoid problems and sidestep pitfalls.

All speaking situations are different. You may be confronted with the need to give a full-length lecture, or you would simply like to put your point of view at a church meeting. Not all of the advice in this book is relevant to every 'speech'. Perhaps only those people who have been asked to give a full-length speech, for example, will need to read the entire section on Practical Techniques. However, whatever the circumstances in which you find yourself mounting the steps to the speaking platform, there is advice here for you. Use the cross-referencing system, the index and the contents pages to find the information you need to start you off on the right foot and help you through.

All speeches begin with a formal address. The appendix on **Forms of Address** is an easy-to-use table which tells you how to address and refer to officials and titled people.

The appendix on **Useful Quotations** is a list of famous and not-so-famous quotations, organized by subject. This list should by no means take the place of a full-scale dictionary of quotations, but it is useful for a quick look up if you need inspiration in a hurry.

Once you have learned the basic tricks of the trade and mastered your nerves, you will find that, far from being an ordeal, speaking in public can be an enjoyable and satisfying experience, and the skills you have aquired will enable you to open up new avenues through which to achieve your personal and professional goals.

ACCEPTING AN INVITATION TO SPEAK

Your best friend is getting married and he has asked you to act as his best man; your boss wants to review the use of database systems in your office and has asked you to present him with a report; you have spent a few weeks in the Himalaya, and a teacher at your child's school asks you to give a slide show to sixth-form students of geography; a work colleague is retiring and you have been asked to present her with a gift and propose a toast.

An invitation to speak in public may come to some like a bolt out of the blue, others are frequently approached to do so. Such an approach may be by way of a formal, written invitation, or at the other end of the scale, an unspoken expectation. Whether you are a professional speaker, a gifted amateur, or simply the obvious choice for the occasion, acceptance of that invitation should never be made without consideration. Leaving aside for the moment questions of blind terror at the mere thought of speaking in public (a reaction that strikes us all, and is dealt with on pp.97–103 Dealing with Nerves), it is useful to find out as much as possible about the occasion and your role in it, before making a decision. This might also be the appropriate moment to find out all you will need to know in order to put together a successful speech.

PRACTICAL TECHNIQUES

Getting the right information

Most events are co-ordinated by a single person, or a small team. In your quest for information, the person to talk to in the first place is the person who extended the invitation, and if he or she cannot answer your questions satisfactorily, ask to talk to somebody else. When you have found the person who is in the know, the questions to which you should have answers break down into two groups: practical questions, which relate to the physical possibility of your being able to attend; and context questions, which give you an idea of the nature of the occasion. The answers to some of the following questions may well be self-evident, however, run through the lists below, and if there is a gap in the information you have been given, try to find someone to answer the question.

Practical questions

A letter of invitation to speak at a formal occasion, for example a dinner or conference, would give basic practical information. If the invitation is verbal, or the written invitation is short on information, get answers to as many of the following questions as possible:

- When and where is the event taking place?
- Find out the day as well as the date so that there is no confusion
- What time are you expected to speak?
- Before lunch, after dinner, at the start or end of the session?
- What is the best way to travel to the venue?
- If you are planning to travel by car, check that there will be a parking space nearby. It is also useful to be given directions, and to have a contact number should you break down on the way. If you are planning to use public transport, check the locations of bus and railway stations, or airports, and ask for or

acquire an up-to-date timetable. Find out whether the organization will be making travel arrangements for you, or whether you are expected to do this yourself.

- Will there be overnight accommodation if necessary?
- You will need to be rested and on top form in order to do yourself justice, and you may need time to relax after you have given your speech. Therefore, if the venue is a fair distance away and you are expected to speak early in the morning or late in the evening, try to arrange accommodation nearby. It is probably preferable to insist on hotel accommodation if you can, being the house guest of a total stranger may add to the stress of the event.
- If you are disabled and require special facilities – wheelchair access, for example – will they be available?
- What dress is required or expected?
- It is important that you do not stick out like a sore thumb (see pp.75–76 **Successful Delivery**), so find out what the form is.
- Is food provided?
- Being confronted with a three-course meal after having just wolfed down a packed lunch may be disconcerting, and by contrast, severe hunger pains and a rumbling stomach may be a distraction you could do without.
- Is there a fee on offer, or can you expect expenses to be reimbursed?

The answers to these questions will tell you whether it is practically possible for you to speak as requested. If all seems to fit in with your schedule and your practical needs, then move on to the second set of questions – about the nature of the event, the expected audience and your role in the proceedings. The answers to the following questions will not only help in making your decision about whether or not to speak, but, if you accept, will also get you well under way with the background information you will need when planning your speech (see pp.10–14 **Setting Objectives**, pp.15–21 **Knowing Your Audience**).

Context questions

These questions fall into three categories: occasion; venue; and audience.

Context questions – occasion

Information about the occasion is vital before you can decide whether or not to accept an invitation to speak.

- What is the occasion?
- Who is the host/host organization?
- Finding out who the host organization is and determining whether or not you are in broad sympathy with their aims and methods will go a long way towards deciding whether or not you want to speak.
- Why are you being asked to speak?
- What do the organizers think are your qualifications for doing the job, and how did they arrive at the decision to invite you in particular?
- What part are you expected to play in the proceedings?
- To propose a toast, to argue a point, to present information, to read a statement? If there are to be a number of speakers, it is particularly important to know exactly what topic you are expected to cover. If you are being asked to speak to a conference of pharmacologists on the latest advances in painkillers, for instance, the organizers will be more than ruffled if you proceed to discuss the use of steroids in international sports.
- Who are the other speakers (if any)?
- A list of names and subjects of other speakers will alert you

to possible overlap which could confuse and bore an audience, and may enable you to confer before the event to prevent this happening. Some idea of the running order may also be useful.

- How long will you be expected to speak for?
- Is this event one in a series?
– If it is part of a series, it is useful to know how the other occasions and speakers have been received by the audience.

Context questions – venue

Further information about the event can be gleaned from questions about the place in which it is being held. The answers to these questions will help when deciding what kind of visual aids and other equipment you may need to use.

- What type of venue is being used?
– This should give you some idea of the kind of speech you are being asked to give. A lecture in a 500-seater conference hall is a different kettle of fish to a slide show in a classroom.
- How will the audience be arranged, and where will you be positioned?
– This tells you how formal the occasion is going to be, and whether elements of audience participation are likely to be successful.
- What kind of equipment is available for visuals?
– Beautifully-prepared overhead projector transparencies are useless if the only equipment at the venue is a slide projector.
- Is there a microphone available, if required?

Context questions – audience

Questions about the audience will not only increase your knowledge of the kind of event you are being asked to participate in, but they will also tell you how much work you will have to do to fit your speech to your audience.

- How large is the audience likely to be?

PRACTICAL TECHNIQUES

- A group of six work colleagues is a far cry from six hundred girl guides.
• Will they be mostly men, women or a mixture of both?
- A bawdy after-dinner speech will not go down too well with an all-female group of churchgoers at a luncheon.
• What age group are they from?
• What is their interest in the proceedings?
- Are they experts or lay people? Will you have to do extra research to bulk out your knowledge of a subject to fit it for an audience of experts, or will you need to spend time explaining techniques and terms that a lay audience may find unfamiliar?
• What do they do for a living?
- What might they be doing if they were not attending this event?
• are they attending on a voluntary or involuntary basis?
- It is going to be harder to hold the interest of a team of telephone sales personnel who would rather spend their time earning their commission than a group of pensioners who regularly attend the event to which you have been invited.
• If this event is part of a series, is the audience significantly the same, and if so, how have they received previous speakers?

Questions of context – occasion, venue and audience – should yield information about the kind of talk you will be expected to give, along with an idea of the overall purpose of the event.

Once you have as much of this information as possible, it is important to consider whether you really are the right person for the job. Don't allow organizers to flatter you into thinking that you are, simply because they have asked you. They could have picked your name out of the telephone directory for all you know! Make sure that you really are expert enough to deliver the goods to this particular audience, but also that you could do so without compromising your principles or insulting the audience. If, on reflection, you feel that you could not discuss the shortcomings of radical feminism without alienating most of the members of the expected audience and starting a riot, you may consider declining (unless that is why you are being invited, of course).

Saying no

Fear of speaking in public is not a good enough reason to refuse an invitation to speak. However, if you have a good reason, saying no should not be difficult. Beware of making flimsy excuses. Many professional conference organizers – or, indeed good club secretaries – are adept at finding their way around an excuse and eventually persuading you to attend!

Perhaps if you have said no on this occasion, but are still keen to learn the skills involved in speech-making, you might consider taking private lessons with a speech teacher, so that next time, you will feel more able to say yes.

Saying yes

So – you are free to speak on the prescribed day, and you are sure that you have something of value to contribute to the proceedings. You have thought the whole proposition through carefully, and you have decided that you would like to accept the invitation to speak.

Whether you have received a written or verbal invitation, it is always a good idea to accept in writing (except in the most informal of circumstances). Include the date, time and venue of the event as you understand them, as a double check.

At this stage, the organizers may ask you to supply a title for your speech, and perhaps a biography for publicity and for the person who introduces you to the audience. Formulating a title is covered in the section on **Planning and Writing** (pp.36–37). A biography should be short and concise, and it should include some personal history, along with a statement of your credentials – the reason why the audience should listen to what you have to say. The whole purpose of your 'introductory' piece is to give confidence to the audience, and this in turn will boost your morale.

A good organizer will confirm your attendance perhaps a week or so in advance, but if this does not happen, call to make sure that practical details have not changed. Do try to check the venue before you speak, especially the acoustics and any equipment you will be using. You may only have the opportunity to do this on the day of your speech (see pp.104–117 **On the Day**),

---

KEY POINTS

√ **think before you accept**
√ **ask practical questions:**
date
time
place
√ **ask context questions:**
occasion
venue
audience
√ **are you the right person for the job?**
√ **only accept if you want to**
√ **if you are keen, but doubt your ability,**
consider seeking advice from a private speech
teacher
√ **accept in writing and confirm closer to the**
event

---

but a 'reconnaissance visit' leaves you time to sort out problems. Knowing that everything is set to go according to plan will help enormously when you are experiencing last-minute nerves.

So the opening salvo has been fired, and the battle is under way. You have committed yourself to speaking to your boss on behalf of departmental colleagues in an effort to have air-conditioning installed; you have agreed to judge the fancy-dress competition at the village fete; you have accepted an invitation to address your local group of bonsai growers.

The next step is to decide what it is you want to say.

SETTING OBJECTIVES

By now you should know a great deal about the speech you have agreed to make. You have double-checked your schedule, you have done your homework on the host organization and they have made their expectations clear. Better still, you have a good idea of the type of audience with which you will be confronted when you rise to your feet to speak. Now is the time to set your objective, to work out what it is you want to achieve in making your speech. A well-formulated statement of objectives will direct your thoughts when you begin to put together your speech. It will also ensure that you end up with a speech that is focused, firmly directed at a clear purpose.

Many expert public speakers use the analogy of making a journey to describe the speech-writing process. In such an analogy, the speech itself is the itinerary, and the audience the people you are planning to take with you. But before anyone mounts an expedition of any sort, they always decide where it is they want to end up – they set their objective.

Regardless of subject, audience or occasion, possible objectives fall into five categories:

- to inspire or to motivate
- to persuade
- to teach or to pass on information
- to explore or to debate ideas
- to entertain

A person is asked to introduce a guest speaker at her company's annual dinner. In doing so, she needs to pass on information about the speaker, motivate the audience to listen to what he or she has to say, and be a little amusing into the bargain. The objectives, therefore, are to **inform**, **motivate** and **entertain**.

A salesperson is meeting representatives of a client firm, and has the task of selling them a product. He needs to persuade them that it is in their interest to buy, but in the process he is quite likely to be putting across information about the product, and it always helps to keep spirits high by amusing the clients at the same time. The objectives are to **persuade**, **inform** and **amuse**.

In these examples, as in most, the speaker lists several of the five categories as objectives. It is always possible, however, to single out one as a primary objective. The others can be termed secondary objectives.

Defining a primary objective

The primary objective is the one that you would aim to achieve in the best of circumstances. It is your main concern when you stand up to speak.

The person charged with introducing a speaker aims to inform, motivate and entertain. The primary objective, however, is to inform. The salesperson would like to persuade, inform and amuse, but the most important part of the task is to persuade. These are the primary objectives for each speaker.

Recognizing the destination

Whether your primary objective is to inform, entertain, persuade, inspire or debate, you should be aiming to provoke either an action or feeling from your audience. If this action or feeling is forthcoming, you have reached your destination – you have succeeded in fulfilling your purpose in speaking. The salesperson's objective is simple; it is to persuade his clients into taking action to buy the product. He knows that he has been successful when they sign the order.

Assessing whether a speech has provoked the hoped-for feeling is a little more difficult, but not impossible. Often a feeling leads to an action of some sort. For example, a sports coach gives a pep-talk to her team before the big match, in an effort to inspire them to feel confident and thus to go on to perform well on the field. She is able to assess the response to her chat by observing the demeanour of her team and their subsequent performance. Experienced speakers learn to assess their audience's reaction to a speech, and to determine whether or not they have succeeded in their objective to provoke a particular feeling.

Setting your objective and working out what action or feeling you would like to provoke is not being suggested so that you are in a position to undertake a post mortem. Just as it is a good idea to know where you are going when you set out on a journey, it helps to direct your thinking to know what it is you want to achieve in making your speech, and it is equally useful to know what the destination looks like. A person going nowhere usually gets there!

Defining secondary objectives

Just as some expeditions never reach their destinations for some reason or another, so too, some speakers fail to attain their primary objective. The salesperson is disappointed when the client does not take the desired action – to buy the product. However, information about the product has been passed on, and the client has had such an entertaining time that relations between the two companies have been much improved. The secondary objectives – to inform and amuse – have been achieved, and so the presentation has not been a total failure.

While secondary objectives are not quite so important as the primary objective (and never settle for second best), it is useful to keep them in mind, as they will give your speech extra depth and substance.

> **Always aim to entertain – at least the audience will have enjoyed listening to you, even if they haven't signed up for a timeshare in the Canary Islands!**

Formulating a statement of objectives

Consider the task you have been given – to speak to a certain audience on a particular occasion about a given subject. Formulate a statement of objectives and write it down in a couple of short sentences. Include your primary and secondary objectives, along with action(s) or feeling(s) you wish to provoke.

The salesperson may formulate a statement of objectives in the following way:

> I am going to persuade ZED Industries to buy our new range of environment-friendly office products. I will inform the company's representatives of the range's special features and keep them amused.

In this statement, the salesperson lists a primary objective (to persuade), along with the action he hopes to provoke (to buy). He then lists two secondary objectives (to inform and to amuse).

When formulating your own statement of objectives, aim for a statement that is concise, simple and positive. It must be possible for you to achieve your objective in the context with which you have been presented, and you should include a 'landmark' by which you will recognize your destination when you reach it.

PRACTICAL TECHNIQUES

When you have formulated your statement of objectives, test it by asking yourself whether it is possible to achieve those ends. Will you really make it to your destination? Is your statement positive, and will you be able to tell whether you have succeeded in your aims? If the answer to any of these questions is no, it is best to reformulate the statement after further thought.

If the answer is yes, it is time to look a little more closely at your travelling companions, and to start putting together an itinerary with them in mind.

KEY POINTS
√ define and formulate your objective
√ identify the required result
√ make your objective possible

KNOWING YOUR AUDIENCE

If there is one golden rule when it comes to speaking in public, it is that one should always keep the audience in mind. Whatever the subject, and regardless of the objectives of the speaker, every speech must meet the expectations of the audience; it must be tailored to suit their needs, interests and level. The wittiest, best-constructed speech ever to be given voice can be the biggest failure if it is given to the wrong audience. Address the audience's needs and engage their interest using language that they will understand, and you have the makings of a successful presentation.

In the section on **Accepting an Invitation** (pp.1–9), it was suggested that among the information to be had from an event organizer is vital intelligence about the audience. The list of useful questions to ask includes:

- Will the audience be made up of mostly men, women, or a mixture of both?
- What age group are they from?
- What is their interest in the proceedings?
- What do they do for a living – how economically successful are they?
- What racial and cultural background do they come from – and what aspirations do they have?
- Are they attending on a voluntary or involuntary basis?

It may also be possible to contact previous speakers to the same audience (for example, if you are asked to take part in a series of lectures), and ask them what they believe to be the salient points about their experience. Add this information to that supplied by the event organizer.

When you are studying the information gathered in these two ways, try to put yourself in the audience's shoes. Try to identify the motivations and aspirations of your group of, say a dozen 20-year-old female students. Characteristics of audiences can be broken down into three areas: their interest; their level of expertise; and their needs.

Audience interest

Every audience that attends an event, be it a shop-floor meeting of departmental members, or an infant's christening party, do so because they have an interest in the proceedings. If you as a speaker can engage that interest, then you will have gone a long way towards grabbing and keeping the audience's attention when you begin to speak.

The audience at a conference may be members of the same profession, and so they have a common interest in staying up-to-date with issues that relate to their business. People attending a meeting to discuss the proposed building of a bypass in their area are either for or against the idea, and the outcome of the meeting may benefit some and not others, but they all have some kind of common interest in the subject under discussion. At a wedding, the audience's sole common interest is usually knowing the families of the bride and groom.

Write down why you think your audience is interested in attending the event at which you will be speaking. Then decide how your subject and your objectives can be reconciled with what you believe your audience's interest to be.

Level of expertise

Each audience can be profiled in terms of its educational background and expertise. Some audiences are drawn from a particular profession, and so, at a lecture on a subject relating to that profession, they would be an expert audience. However, put the same people in a workshop on quilting, and they may become a lay, or non-expert audience. You may be an expert in bookbinding, but if you are speaking to an audience of booksellers, you may well have to explain the technical terms you use, and limit the amount of information you supply so that they understand fully what it is you are talking about.

Most audiences, however, are mixed in terms of their expertise. In this case, it would be foolish to commit yourself to a subject that you have to discuss in such general terms for the sake of the layman, that the experts would consider attending a complete waste of time. If you do so, you would fail to attain your objectives as described in the previous section. It would be better to choose a subject that can be discussed successfully before as many members of the audience as possible, a subject that they can all understand, and in which they all have an interest.

Of course, if your objective is primarily to entertain (for example, if you are speaking after dinner), then questions of expertise become secondary. However, you will still need to assess your audience's background in order to pitch your anecdotes and references at the correct level.

Write down what you think your audience's level of expertise is likely to be, and then decide how this will affect your speech. You may have to make a speech designed for experts more general so that lay people can understand, you may have to define your terms and adopt a didactic approach. Alternatively, you may have to look for an altogether different approach to the subject that can be presented to a mixed audience in order to achieve the objectives you have formulated.

PRACTICAL TECHNIQUES

Meeting the needs of the audience

Every audience has its 'expertise profile', and its own interest in attending the event. Join an audience in its common interest (if there is one) and speak to it in terms it can understand, and you are well on your way towards achieving your objectives. However, the real key to winning an audience's attention and making them ready to listen, is to understand their needs and incorporate them into your speech.

Psychologists believe that modern-day people have a number of needs, and that these needs are basically the same for everyone:

- Economic – the need to be financially better off or secure.
- Physical comfort – the need to be warm and fed, but also to be unconfined, to be free to roam.
- Psychological – the need to be free from worry and psychological anxiety.
- Acceptance – the need to feel that other people accept them as part of a social group.
- Exploration – the need to know and understand new facts and concepts.
- Political security – the need to be free from political constraint.

Each member of an audience comes to an event with all of these needs. They expect the speaker to fulfil at least one of these needs, or to tell them something that may help them to do so. Identifying the audience's particular needs, and speaking with them in mind will gain the audience's attention (by making them think that you have something of value to say), and keep their interest (by relating what you are saying to their most deep-seated needs). It is vital that you fulfil the audience's expectations if your speech is to be a success.

Take the example of a group of local residents meeting to discuss council plans for the building of a bypass. They have a single common area of interest (the bypass), and they are probably of mixed expertise. Their needs in this case are probably exploration needs (to find out about the bypass) and physical comfort needs (to ensure that their physical comfort is not compromised). On another level, they are also hoping to look after their economic needs (their property may fall in value as a result of a nearby bypass) and psychological needs (they would like to have their minds put at rest that their other needs will be fulfilled by future events).

If you were speaking to this group on either side – arguing for or against the bypass – your speech will be all the more persuasive if you centre your arguments around the needs of the audience. Arguing that the bypass is in the interests of the country as a whole – it adds to the improvement of the country's infrastructure, etc. – is not as immediate to this audience as arguing that traffic will be diverted away from their area, and therefore their lives will be improved. Identify with the audience's needs directly in this way and you will find them sympathetic and attentive.

If you perceive a group to have mixed needs, then you should try to speak to as many of those needs as possible, just as you should try to speak to an audience of mixed expertise in terms that all members can understand or will find stimulating.

For example, a member of a company's management team is trying to implement some changes to working systems. She is speaking to a group of representatives from both management and workforce. All of these people have exploration needs, and so she incorporates as much information as possible on the proposed system. However, each person also has other needs, and these needs vary depending on where each individual stands in the company hierarchy. In order to gain their attention (and in this case, to attain the objective of persuading them to agree to implement her working system), she must speak to some if not all of these needs.

Members of management will in general be looking to achieve savings in time and money, increases in productivity and improvement in the quality of the product. On the other hand, a member of the shop-floor workforce will be motivated by other factors: the safeguarding of pay levels and conditions; and the maintenance of job satisfaction and job security. If the speaker can show that she has considered most if not all of these needs, then she will have the attention and sympathetic ear of most members of her audience. If she is completely successful, all members of the audience will go away with the feeling that it would be a good idea to implement the new systems because there is something in it for them.

Decide how a discussion of your chosen subject will meet the needs of your particular audience. Consider why you think that the audience should spend time listening to you, when they could be doing something else. What do you have to say that it is in their interest to hear?

Now to assemble everything you know about your audience, putting together your perceptions about their interest in attending, their level of expertise and their needs. Go back to the statement of your own objectives in speaking to them. In the light of your deeper knowledge of the audience, ask yourself whether you still think you will reach your destination with this particular group of travelling companions in tow. Perhaps you will need to take a level path that is not too circuitous in order for your fellow travellers to keep up with you. Or you may decide to take the scenic route to keep them interested in the journey. Alternatively, you may find that your audience is quite willing and able to jog up the mountainside with you before breakfast!

When you have successfully married the needs and level of your audience with your stated objectives, you have completed the pre-planning work vital to constructing a good speech. The next stage is to plan the speech itself, keeping the audience, its needs and expectations, firmly in mind.

KEY POINTS

√ **always keep the audience in mind**
√ **analyse their interest in the subject**
√ **define the audience's needs**
√ **speak with their interest and needs uppermost**
√ **reconcile your own objectives with the needs of the audience**

GENERAL RESEARCH

Good research is one of the keys to good speech-preparation, and more than that, an audience will look on a speaker who has done his or her research with infinitely more respect than on one who has clearly done very little, and as a consequence has nothing of substance to say. However talented and experienced you may be, a successful speech is created through 1% inspiration and 99% perspiration. Therefore, take your research seriously.

You may have to do a little or a lot of research to amass enough information for your speech, depending on the type of speech you are going to be making. You may be giving a business or political speech, in which case, you will need to gather as many facts and figures as possible – ammunition with which to argue your cause. On the other hand, you may be speaking at a social occasion, in which case the information content of your speech may be considerably less, but you may need a number of anecdotes and jokes, cleverly spaced throughout your speech, to keep your audience amused.

Sources of information and other ammunition

Whatever type of speech they specialize in, and whatever their subject matter, most successful public speakers are obsessive hoarders of information, anecdotes, jokes and observations. If you plan to speak in public on a regular basis, then you should do the same. If you do, you will find that not only do you have a good stock of ready ammunition when it comes to writing your speech, but you will also find that you have a lot more to say for yourself in day-to-day conversation.

Ammunition can come from a number of sources. Here are a few to cultivate:

● **newspapers and magazines**
Read a national newspaper regularly, especially the pages relating to subjects in your field of interest. Depending on your subject, you will soon find the newspaper that provides the best coverage. Take the trade magazine, if there is one, and scan newsstand magazines for general interest. Never overlook the local press, even free newspapers – they can tell you a great deal about local issues and opinion. Cut out articles that could be useful, or simply snippets that amuse you and might amuse your audience. Humorous misprints are particularly useful, as are short reports of unusual events and happenings. Write the date and source on your clippings, and file them according to subject.

● **broadcast media**
Keep a notebook next to the television or radio, so that you can jot down anything that could be useful.

● **libraries**
The local library may be your first port of call when you begin to research a subject, and most hold many of the reference books you cannot afford to buy. Librarians can also be helpful in putting you in touch with local groups and associations, and bulletin boards will tell you a lot about what is happening in your local area. If you need books that your local library does not hold, ask for the inter-library loan service – although this can take time, especially if you need books that are only held at the large central or university libraries, it may be the only way to get your hands on the type of information you need. Most libraries

also hold back copies of newspapers and magazines, and some have periodical indexes, to enable you to find articles recently published on your subject. Ask whether your library keeps back copies of newspapers and magazines on microfilm. If you have a university or polytechnic near you, it may be possible for you to become a member, usually on payment of a one-off or annual fee.

● **reference books**
Access to good reference books is a necessity – smoothing the path of anyone wishing to put together a speech. Here are a number that are invaluable:

English Dictionary
Vital. There are many on the market, the main rivals being Chambers, Collins and Oxford. All dictionaries are not the same – for example, Collins is the most modern, and contains more slang and jargon, but the Oxford includes more of the less-common words. Browse before you buy – a concise should be large enough for most people's needs.

Thesaurus
Gives synonyms and alternatives for a large number of words. The word you have in mind is found in an index at the back of the book, and you are then referred to a main entry, which gives alternatives. The most famous is Roget's Thesaurus. Use it to find alternatives for those overworked everyday words.

Whittacker's Almanac
An annual publication that is packed with diverse information, from a list of events taking place in the current year, to the names of all the peers of the realm. It also includes: political, economic and geographical information on all the countries of the world: a

list of international organizations from the General Council of the United Nations to the South Pacific Commission, giving their addresses and functions: a list of British specialist associations; weights and measures, with metric to imperial conversion charts; lists of historic monuments and museums by region. A veritable mine of information, it is up to date, and the paperback is relatively cheap.

Dictionary of Phrase and Fable
There are several on the market, but the oldest and most famous is Brewer's. Originally written by Dr Ebenezer Cobham Brewer in 1870, it has recently been updated. Ebenezer himself called it 'a Treasury of Literary Bric à Brac'. It lists such things as mythological names, the signs of the Zodiac, proverbs, and words and phrases ancient and current. The cross-referencing system is a delight, and it is excellent for providing inspiration.

Book of Dates
Another source of inspiration, a book that lists each day of the year, tells you who was born, who died and what events took place on that day. Use it to tie your speech to the day it is to be given: 'Today is the 45th anniversary of the birth of Joe Bloggs...'

Guinness Book of Records
A fascinating resource from which to pick relevant facts and figures to spice up a speech. It is usefully arranged by subject, and, because it is revised annually, you can always rely on its information being up-to-date. If you have time to browse in a bookshop, you may find other collections of miscellaneous and offbeat facts – often in the children's section.

PRACTICAL TECHNIQUES

Biographical Dictionary
Gives details of famous people; a necessity for checking full names, life dates and other information.

Book of Quotations
Again, there are many books of quotations on the market. Look for one that is organized by theme rather than by author, for quicker access to relevant quotes. Try to find one that gives some detail on the author, that is, life dates and a description of what they did. If you have one of these, you will not need to refer to the biographical dictionary so often. If you do decide to buy a book of quotations, don't rely on it as a sole source. Continue to collect quotations and witticisms yourself, perhaps using the list at the end of this book as a starting point.

Encyclopedia
The entire Encyclopaedia Britannica is not necessary, but you will probably find a concise encyclopedia useful for checking facts. There are several relatively cheap encyclopedias on the market.

● **general reading**
Most good speakers are avid readers. Biographies are particularly useful. When reading anything at all, look up words that are new to you, and jot down their meanings. Perhaps if you find that your vocabulary is particularly limited – if you often find yourself casting around for the right word – you might consider using a small notebook to keep new words and their meanings together, so that you actively increase your word power.

● **the host organization**
In the section on **Accepting an Invitation** (p.1) it was made clear that the host organization is a vital contact for information on the event at which you plan to speak, and the expected audi-

26

ence. However, your host can also supply other kinds of information. If it is a company, they may have an annual report which will tell you the company's perceptions on the state of the industry and its share of the market, as well as providing invaluable information on the company's activities. If your host is a local club or association, ask if they put out a newsletter that could be useful. If you are expecting to propose a toast, or to give a keynote speech, then the host organization should be able to supply you with a list of the names of the people you should mention.

● **experts**
It may be necessary to contact experts in the field you are researching. Most are quite willing to discuss a point, or to give advice as to where to find the information you need. Try the relevant university departments – it may be a good idea to explain your situation to the registrar's office, and to ask to be given the name of someone who might help. Associations and institutes may also be able to put you in touch with expert members who may be willing to help. If you have read an interesting article in a magazine and need further information, write to the author care of the magazine's editorial offices. Don't be shy – most experts are flattered that you are interested in their subject, and will do everything in their power (time permitting) to ensure that you have the facts straight – it is in their interests to do so, after all.

● **specialist associations**
There are associations and institutes to cover almost any subject you chose to name. Most of these are willing to supply information, and some will put you in touch with members, or suggest other places to find out what you need to know. Whittacker's Almanac, an annual publication listed along with other useful reference books above, gives a comprehensive list of names and addresses.

PRACTICAL TECHNIQUES

• other speakers
Attend as many events as possible, especially if you plan to cover a specialist area. Note down useful anecdotes and turns of phrase, interesting openings and successful jokes. When you recycle such material, however, be careful to fit it to your own audience, but more importantly, make sure that you are not committing plagiarism (see p.30).

• conversations and hearsay
Get into the habit of talking to people; many conversations will yield useful anecdotes and information. Carry a notebook so that you can jot things down, and don't be afraid to do so in public! It is obviously a good idea to ask whether you can use an anecdote heard in conversation, and to check any facts that you may be given before you use them. Learn the art of listening, and cultivate the kind of people who know what is happening, especially if you plan to be speaking in the local government arena.

Filing your material
Research filing systems vary widely: from a number of shoe boxes stacked in the corner, to paper files, brown envelopes, or computer databases. Whatever your system, it is important to sort items of interest into subject area. In doing so, you will have thought a little about the use each item could be put to, and you will remember what you have much more easily.

When stocking your arsenal, always date your snippets, and note down the source for future reference. You will then know whether the information you have is out of date, and you will be alerted to the fact that you may have to check facts gathered, say, from conversations.

Staying in touch
All good journalists keep a contact book – a list of the names and addresses of people who can supply you with information and

advice. If you decide to compile a contact book, keep it separate from your personal address book, and make notes on each person's position and specialist field.

Checking the facts

If you plan to be speaking in public regularly, keeping an eye out for ammunition all the time is a must. When you come to putting together your speech, however, it is vital that you check and double check your facts. Once a speaker has patently made an error of fact, his or her reliability will be called into question, and the audience will not forget even a single lapse. Everything you say after the initial error will be tarred with the same brush, and the audience will remain forever sceptical.

When using statistics or figures, check them, and when you use them, quote your sources. If you are using a quotation, five seconds looking it up in a reference book – checking the exact wording and the source – will save you the shame of being corrected in public. If you intend to use visuals of any sort that require you to spell words you are not too sure about, check them and write them down somewhere, so that you are sure to get it right on the day.

Avoiding slander

When a person commits slander against another, they say something in public about them that is untrue, and with intent to harm their reputation in some way. When discussing other people's activities, therefore, check your facts three times over. Ensure that what you say is unlikely to harm their reputation in any way. Many defendants in slander cases have found themselves in trouble not because they intended to harm a person's reputation, but because they simply got their facts wrong. In any case, speaking ill of other people in public is not good form, and should be avoided in the same way as remarks in bad taste.
If in doubt – leave it out!

PRACTICAL TECHNIQUES

Plagiarism

Plagiarism is the appropriation of the words or ideas of another person. It can range from quoting from somebody else and not citing the source, to appropriating entire speeches and trying to pass them off as one's own. Plagiarism should be avoided at all costs – it is a crime that is easily discovered, and substantiated charges of plagiarism against you will ruin your credibility as a speaker.

If you want to use other people's words, try as often as possible to cite the source – 'I read the following words in *The Times* leader column today . . .', 'To quote the words of George Washington . . .', 'At a function last week, one of the guests told me a story, which I would like to relate to you . . .'. If you intend to recycle an anecdote, always rearrange it to fit your context. In this way you will avoid charges of plagiarism and keep your audience interested at the same time.

Never lift entire arguments from another speaker. You may one day find yourself on the platform with that same speaker, about to give an all-too-familiar speech, or you may find that the audience has heard that speaker on a previous occasion, and, having heard it all before, will give you a cool response. Worse still, the original speaker may give a speech, only to discover that the audience has already heard your plagiarized version a week previously. In these cases, it is all too easy to point a finger at you the culprit, and you may well find yourself *persona non grata* as a result.

Apart from the ever-present fear of discovery, there is a second, and perhaps more compelling reason for never repeating (verbatim or not) the arguments or line of thought of another speaker. Your speech should be unique. It should have been honed to fit the audience, the context and the venue. It should include up-to-the-minute information and, most importantly, your own original thinking. Dusting off somebody else's speech to present to another audience in a completely different context will produce nothing but failure.

OFFICIAL SECRETS ACT

Warning – if your subject area may be in any way sensitive under the Official Secrets Act, get advice.

KEY POINTS

√ **sources of ammunition**
media – newspapers, magazines, radio, TV
libraries
reference books
general reading
your host
experts
specialist associations
other speakers
in conversation

√ **file it**
√ **check the facts**
√ **avoid slander and plagiarism**

Bringing together the information

You have been keeping an eye on the media, and you have already acquired an amount of information on your given subject. The next section shows how to update the general research you have amassed, and begin to plan and write your speech.

PLANNING AND WRITING

> Seek not for words, seek only fact and thought,
> And crowding in will come the words
> unsought.
>
> **Horace**

You are sitting at your kitchen table, or at your office desk, with a blank piece of paper in front of you, pen in hand. You stare at the paper, desperately searching for a good way to open your speech. You have an idea in your mind of the kind of people you are going to be speaking to, and you know what you want to achieve by doing so, but still that opening sentence will not come to mind. STOP! The reason that you are finding it so difficult is that you are starting in the wrong place. The previous section described how to start and maintain ongoing general research files – the hallmark of a serious public speaker. But now, you must first clarify your subject and do a little more specific research before planning and eventually writing your speech.

As soon as you know the general subject of your speech, start a new file. Look through the other files and notebooks you have amassed, and pull out anything that might be relevant. Read each snippet to refresh your memory of it. Write the subject of your proposed speech on the front of the new file and put all those pieces of paper into it. Now, you may find that you have to do some more specific research – gathering up-to-date facts and

figures or checking them, finding out a little bit more about your host organization, contacting fellow speakers, etc.

How much information is enough?

As a general rule, too much research is better than too little. You will probably throw out most of the material at the planning stages, but it is important that you have it under your belt, if for no other reason than to give you the confidence that comes from knowing as much as you can about the subject under discussion.

Using personal experience

Your research should be a process of discovery, not only of cold facts and other people's arguments, but also of your own relevant experiences and feelings. Relating these will enable you to inject the personal touch into your speech, and it will probably do much to inspire the enthusiasm necessary to be able to transmit a strong message to your audience. Search your mind for memories of events and your reactions to them. Write these down and add them to your subject file. If you have read an article, decide whether or not you agree with the author, and if you don't, work out why you don't. Make a note. File it away.

Fermenting ideas

Only part of the capacity of the human brain is engaged in conscious thought. Waking or sleeping, a great part of your brain is subconsciously mulling over ideas and experiences, gently fermenting them, analyzing and synthesizing all the time, while your conscious mind takes care of other things. This is why many of us have ideas or remember events long since past at odd times of the day or night – in the bath, driving to work, in the middle of the night, carrying home the groceries.

Reflect on the subject in the days and weeks of your planning period. Keep going back to your file and looking over the pile of information that is growing there. Put it in the back of your mind. Allow the subconscious part of your brain time to shuffle the information you are collecting, and you will find that connections will begin to pop into your head, apparently from nowhere. Carry a notebook with you, and write down any thoughts that come to mind at such odd moments. Add them to your mountain of material.

This process of fermentation is quite time-consuming, however, remember that most of the work is being done by a part of the brain that you do not normally use in day-to-day life, and so by adopting this process, you are in effect doubling your thinking time.

About a week before you are due to give your speech, return to your desk or kitchen table – it is time to put in some conscious effort.

Selecting and arranging the material

At this stage it would be a mistake to simply sit down with research material scattered about you, and try to begin to write. A successful speech utilizes a relatively small amount of information, chosen for its relevance to the audience and for its usefulness in achieving the objectives of the speaker.

Different people have different methods of planning their speeches. Most, however, engage in some form of brainstorming, in which they scribble down on a large piece of paper in no particular order all the ideas and information that comes into their head. When you are doing this, look through the subject research files you have compiled and add anything that you may have forgotten. Look over your scribbles, and begin to connect one with another.

Soon, a train of thought will become apparent, items of information will link themselves to particular lines of argument, and some material will assume greater or lesser importance in comparison with other material. Quotations and anecdotes will find their logical uses by relating themselves to particular points in the argument.

Defining the topic

Speech-writing is a process of simplification rather than elaboration. If you have followed through the advice given on research and fermenting ideas, you will probably find that you are faced with a plethora of material – too much by far to deliver to an involuntary audience in five minutes flat!

So far, what you have is material on a particular subject, but you will now need to whittle it down until you have a small, well-defined topic upon which to speak. Do this by writing down words or a phrase that covers the subject you want to tackle. Now write a list of the topics that fall into this subject field. Choose the one that you feel most relates to your audience's needs and expectations, and is most likely to enable you to fulfil your objectives. Again, write down a list of sub-topics under your chosen topic heading, and choose one that fits with the context (audience needs and your objectives).

A speaker is asked to talk to a group of undergraduate students on the media. The process of choice and elimination goes on until she has come to a defined topic on which to speak, as follows:

The general subject of **media** can be broken down into television, radio, magazines and newspapers. The topic of **newspapers** can be further broken down into their coverage: home news, foreign news, sport, features (lifestyle, women's pages, gossip columns) and comment. The sub-topic of **foreign news** can be divided into war, natural disasters and politics. Again, the

35

sub-topic of **war** coverage can be broken down into censorship and propaganda.

At this stage the speaker calls a halt, and decides that the topic for her speech should be: propaganda as it appears in coverage of foreign wars in the national press.

The topic is well-defined, and concise enough to cover in the time given. It will enable the speaker to impart some information, and debate issues, but also to fulfil the exploration needs of her semi-expert audience.

Once you have a concise definition of the topic you wish to cover, rearrange your material under headings that fit in with that topic. Cut away any superfluous material, information that does not relate directly to the given subject. Each of your headings should reflect a single train of thought. Number each heading in a running order from the least to the most important. As you group the material under these headings, prioritize each snippet, make one follow another in a logical argument.

Composing a title

Some organizers, especially of lectures, require that you let them have a title in advance of giving your speech. This is so that they can include it in their programme and publicity material. When you have defined your topic and sorted the information you have into a rough idea of what you want to say, you should be able to think about a title.

Your title should be short and to the point. It should in no way be enigmatic or mysterious – say exactly what the subject of your speech is. 'The Philosophy of René Descartes' is better than 'I think, therefore I am', for instance. However, you might like to make use of the style of title that has a double-barrel, so to speak, giving an enigmatic 'catch' and then an explanation. For example, a lecture about the Irish author Flann O'Brien might be titled: 'The Hard Life: The work and life of Flann O'Brien'. A talk on how to assert yourself in the workplace could go under the title, 'Speak for Yourself: Self-assertion techniques for company employees'. The lecturer on propaganda in the press in the previous example might entitle her speech, 'Foreign Foes: propaganda in the national press'.

Try to make your title catchy, and to make your speech sound interesting, rather than deathly dull – the aim is, after all, to entice people to come to hear you speak!

Structuring a speech

A good speech is pieced together in a defined structure, and contains a number of specific elements. To use a time-honoured analogy, each speech is created as flesh covering a skeleton. The bones of the skeleton have a specific purpose, and material must be chosen that fulfils that purpose. The skeleton of a speech is as follows:

● The opening: in which the speaker needs to grab the attention of the audience, and tell them why it is worthwhile to listen.

● Introduction to the subject: in which the speaker gives an overview of the material to be covered.

● The body of the speech: in which the speaker presents information or arguments.

● Close: in which the speaker draws conclusions from the information already presented, and leaves the audience with something to think about.

It is widely held that any composition, including a speech, has a beginning, a middle and an end. However, speeches are not written essays, they are spoken presentations. The most important difference between the two is that a speech is fleeting, it is uttered and then disappears. When a reader is distracted from the text, or becomes confused, he or she can turn back the page and re-read. But, it is not possible for listeners to do this, and so you as the speaker must do it for them. The good speech-writer builds in a number of elements so that the audience not only stays awake, but also follows what is being said, and if the speech is successful, exhibits the desired feeling or action. These elements are:

• Splashes: attention grabbers, with which to engage the interest of the audience at the start of the speech, and wake them up when they begin to doze off.

• Appeals: sentences that identify the speaker's purpose with the needs of the audience, and thus convince them that he or she has something of value to say.

• Links: sentences that link one piece of the argument to the next in a logical manner. The links could be seen as the sinews that hold the bones together.

WRITING TIP

It is generally easier to write the introduction and body of your speech before you tackle the opening and the close. You will write a more effective opening and close if you deal with them together at the end of the writing process.

● Summaries and repetitions: useful techniques to ensure that the audience follows the argument and remembers as much as possible after you have stepped out of the limelight. The general rule is: tell them what you are going to tell them; tell them; and then tell them what you have told them.

Openings

When a speaker rises to begin speaking, the audience first of all appraises him or her on physical appearance, and second on the words uttered in the first few moments. (The effect of physical appearance is covered in **Successful Delivery** on pp.74–82.) This is a rare moment in which the speaker has the undivided attention of the audience. They are waiting to be told if the speaker is worth listening to, and they will make their decision in the first few moments. Now is the time to tell them why they should bother continuing to listen.

Apart from the formal address (see **Forms of Address** p.247), the elements to build into an opening are: a splash, an appeal and credentials, followed by a statement of the topic on which you are going to speak.

The splash is a method of grabbing the audience's attention. It could be a pointed question, an interesting fact, a surprising or shocking statistic, a short joke or anecdote, or a lively (perhaps funny) quotation. Choose a splash that is topical and relevant.

Once the audience is paying attention, make them see that your subject is not only interesting but also relevant to their experience and needs. Identify with your audience's needs as you perceive them.

Next, prove to the audience that you are someone who has something worthwhile to say, and that your facts can be relied upon. State your credentials, then give a short, simple explanation of what it is you are going to talk about, and what you hope to achieve by doing so. These last two elements, the statement of the subject and of your objectives should be in effect a promise to go some way towards fulfilling the audience's needs.

Here is an example of an opening that incorporates these elements. A speaker is addressing a mixed-gender local group about personal safety:

'In the last three months, eleven people have been mugged, raped or assaulted in this area. That's nearly one person a week. And at some time or other we have all, men as well as women, felt vulnerable when walking home late at night. In any event, the chances are that we will have to face this danger at some time. And whatever our personal experience, we would all feel a lot better if we knew we were doing all we could to reduce the risk of being attacked.

For 12 years now, I've given courses across the country in personal safety, and I'm here to give you some tips on how to reduce the danger of attack, and how best to deal with potentially dangerous situations. My aim is not to teach self-defence, but simply to enable you to feel more secure when you are walking in the street at night.'

ELEMENTS OF AN OPENING

- **make a splash to grab audience attention**
- **appeal to needs**
- **give credentials**
- **state the topic**
- **state your aims**

The speaker gets to her feet and engages the audience's attention with a shocking statistic. This is the initial splash. She then immediately identifies with the audience's needs by mentioning

a common experience. She gives her credentials – 12 years running courses on personal safety – and then states her theme
(avoiding danger on the streets), along with her objective (to
make members of the audience feel more secure).

A strong opening should be confident, friendly, short and
simple. The speaker who apologizes for not being the world's
expert on the subject will never win the audience's respect.
Equally, a long, rambling opening will confuse and irritate,
boding no good for the rest of the speech. Remember that you
may well be suffering from nerves, so make your opening lines
easy to get right.

Introducing the subject

When you have finished arranging all your material, you should
have a series of headings that lead from one another in a logical
order. Under each of these headings you will have a number of
pieces of material to utilize. During the introduction, you need
to lay out for the audience the bare bones of your argument, the
stage in which you are going to present your material. State each
of the headings in the order in which you are going to present
them, and explain what they mean. Tell the audience what it is
that you are going to tell them.

A director of a small firm is experiencing difficulties with his
staff. He has called a meeting of his partners to discuss ways in
which he can improve employee standards. His introduction of
the substance of his presentation might, therefore, go like this:

'The problems that we are facing when it comes to staff seem to
fall into three categories: poor recruitment; insufficient in-house
training; and too little funding for refresher courses. I would like
to take each of these issues in turn, and put forward some ways in
which we might tackle them.'

PRACTICAL TECHNIQUES

The director has broken down his material into three sections, and tells his audience what these sections are. He has also given some idea of the kind of thing he is going to be saying about each ('to put forward some ways in which we might tackle them'). In one or two sentences, he has sketched out the shape for his presentation.

If the speaker were presenting a more complicated subject, perhaps to a lay audience, he or she might have to explain a little about each heading, to ensure that the audience understands immediately what is being said. A speaker is introducing a slide show on a journey through Spain:

'The journey was carried out in three stages. We landed at the city of Barcelona in the east, which is the capital of the province of Catalonia. We then travelled cross-country to Castille, heading from Spain's capital, Madrid. The third leg of the journey took us south to Andalucia, to visit the historic cities of Cordoba, Seville and Granada before returning home.'

The speaker is defining three stages to his presentation: first Barcelona and Catalonia, second the journey to Madrid, and third, the Andalucian cities. He has said a little about each, so that the names of these perhaps unfamiliar places are illuminated.

By sketching out the shape of the speech to come, the speaker is giving the audience some idea of how long the road to the destination is, and what landmarks are along the way. In this way, the listeners know how to pace themselves, and what to look out for as they near the destination.

The body of the speech
Having persuaded the audience to come along on the journey, and told them the route and how long it is going to take them to get there, the speaker steps out on the first stage towards the

destination. He or she presents each piece of material under the first heading – advice, perhaps, or information and opinion – and when this is exhausted, goes on to the next. The gap between one stage and the next is bridged with a link – a sentence or two that act as a springboard from which to leap from one side of the divide to the other.

'We were sad to leave the cosmopolitan city of Barcelona, most especially its wonderful cuisine. But next day, we began the journey west towards Madrid, looking forward to seeing the many famous sights of this, the capital of all Spain.'

This link leads from the part of the journey which has already been described to the next part. In doing so, the speaker reminds the audience of what he found to be the most memorable experience of Barcelona – its cuisine – and why the next destination should be something to look forward to.

The company director in the example on page 41 might link sections in the following way:

'If we tackle the problem of poor recruitment in the ways I have put forward, we should find ourselves with a staff that is capable of providing us with the skills we need. But, however well-qualified they may be when they first join us, we will still need to train them in our house systems.'

Once again, the speaker has referred back to what has gone before, and then used a linking sentence to bridge the gap between the first and second stages of the argument.

It is possible to present any number of stages in an argument or discussion in this way. However, the more stages there are, the more likely it is that the audience will become lost or bored. Make sure that at every bridging point you use a strong link sentence, which looks back to the sections already discussed, and then makes the leap to the next.

The company director has now finished discussing in-house training for new staff members, and wants to go on to his last point, about sending staff on refresher courses.

'Recruiting competent staff and training them to do things our way is all well and good. But this industry is moving so fast that it is imperative that we stay ahead of our competitors by investing a small amount of money keeping our staff's skills up-to-the-minute with the latest technology.'

The speaker has not only looked back to the section immediately preceding, but he has also reminded his partners of the first of the three phases of the argument. Accumulating and enumerating the parts of the argument as you go along helps the audience not only to see where they are going, but also to remember where they have been. You are helping them to orientate themselves in a foreign country.

When putting together the body of the speech, don't forget to maintain the audience's interest, by appealing to their needs, especially at link points. Remind them why they should continue to listen. You understand that they want to make money, to improve their knowledge or their physical well-being, and if they continue to listen they will hear still more to their advantage!

In the example above, the director is making the link between in-house training and refresher courses by appealing to his partners' need to make money by staying ahead of the competition. Ideally each stage of your speech should appeal to the audience's needs, and during link passages, you should take the opportunity to give voice to this appeal.

WRITING TIP

Remember the formula:
Tell them what you are going to tell them.
Tell them.
Tell them what you have told them.

Closing the speech

Most audiences have very short concentration spans. They are attentive at the start of a presentation, but after a few minutes their concentration begins to flag. However, just like footsore travellers, they begin to perk up again when the destination is sighted on the horizon. Point out the destination to the audience – tell them that you are beginning to draw your conclusions. If you manage to claim their attention in this way, the close of the speech becomes just as important as the opening, because it too is an opportunity to lodge your argument in your listeners' memories.

The close should include a short summary of all the material you have covered in your presentation, and you should draw any conclusion from the arguments you have presented. In this way you will repeat for a third time the salient points that you wished to put across, and the audience is likely to remember some of what you have said. If you are trying to persuade your audience to some form of action, enjoin them to do what you want them to in your closing words.

Always end on a high note, and try to leave the audience with words that sum up your speech. Anecdotes, jokes, rhetorical questions or quotations are always good ways to end.

Above all, make sure that you close confidently – let the audience know that you have finished speaking. Never use words to

PRACTICAL TECHNIQUES

the effect of 'Well that's all I have to say . . .' or 'I seem to have
come to the end of my notes, so that's it . . .'. A firm 'thank-you'
is good enough for many occasions, and most audiences respond
to these words with a round of applause.

KEY POINTS

✓ compile as much research as you can
✓ allow ideas to ferment
✓ define the topic; limit the field
✓ work to a clear structure:
opening
introduction
body
close
✓ make use of:
splashes
appeals
links
repetition

IMPROVING YOUR STYLE

> Wit is a sword; it is meant to make people
> feel the point as well as see it.
>
> G. K. Chesterton

The ease and wit that make many professional
speakers so entertaining is, in most cases,
developed over many years on the circuit. While
the best speakers are endowed with a significant
talent for communication, it would be a mistake to
believe that good speaking is something that
cannot be learned. On the contrary, follow a few
general rules, and pay attention to some specific
points of style, and with practise it is quite possible
for anyone to become a good speaker.

The following guidelines apply to a speech
written out in full. Experienced speakers may skip
this part of the process and extemporize from a set
of headings and a few memory-joggers. In a later
section, it will be explained how to condense a
speech into a series of notes, rather than read it
word for word. Although composing a speech in
full is a time-consuming process, for
inexperienced speech-makers, however, it can help
to mould a jumble of ideas into a well-argued
presentation and give the confidence that comes
from knowing exactly what you are going to say
before you have to say it.

Three general rules to bear in mind when
putting into words the ideas you want to convey
are: converse with your audience; be yourself; keep
it simple.

PRACTICAL TECHNIQUES

A public conversation

The most constructive way to think of your speech is as a conversation, albeit ordered, one-sided and with a larger number of people than usual. When you are putting words onto paper, keep an image of the audience in mind, and write as if you were speaking. It may help to say some sentences out loud as you write, just to try out the sound.

Listen to spoken conversations of all kinds, and not the differences between written and spoken English. For example, most native English speakers rarely say 'do not'. Instead, they almost always contract it to 'don't', except when adding emphasis. The same goes for 'won't', 'can't', 'wouldn't', etc. While most of us were taught at school never to use these contractions in written compositions, it is a positive aid to do so when putting together a speech.

Incorporate the kinds of words and phrases that you would use in everyday speech. By all means, work to extend your vocabulary by wide reading and frequent use of the dictionary, but employ the new words you have learned only when the context dictates. Use formal language only in the few circumstances that call for it. Feel free to break the rules of written English – few people speak the way our school teachers would have us write.

Be yourself

A golden rule when speaking in public – or in any conversational situation for that matter – is to be yourself. The audience has come to hear **YOU** speak, and just as using your own experiences and opinions will add to the substance of your speech, so your personal way of using the English language will go a long way towards creating a genuinely original style.

Never succumb to the temptation to emulate the speaking styles of other people, unless of course you are quoting or relating an anecdote that calls for characterization (and never do this unless you are certain you can carry it off). Audiences are capable of seeing through artificial personas, and they will lose their respect for you as a speaker if they come to believe that you are shamming.

**A GOOD SPEECH EXHIBITS
THREE CHARACTERISTICS:**

- **clarity – keep it simple**
- **enthusiasm – make it personal**
- **novelty – ensure it is original**

Keep it simple

Don't try to be too clever in your speaking. Audiences want to grasp quickly and easily what you are trying to tell them. They are not interested in how many syllables you can string together, or whether your command of the subjunctive is impeccable. Keep sentences short and to the point. Each sentence should represent a single step along the way.

Excessively formal or complex sentence constructions, along with unnecessary obtuseness will only confuse and bore. Your overriding aim as a speaker should always be to communicate, rather than to impress. Say what you mean – no more and no less.

As you are writing, test your work to ensure that you have complied with these three general style rules. Ask yourself:

PRACTICAL TECHNIQUES

- Do people use these words in conversation?
- Are these the words I would normally use to express this?
- Is this paragraph/sentence free of unnecessary words?

If the answer to all of these questions is yes, you have the basis of a style that is accessible, personal and palatable.

Good style is based on the desire to communicate. The following advice on specific points of style will, if followed, improve your ability to get the message across, and to make sure that the audience remembers as much as possible of the material you are presenting.

ONE THOUGHT AT A TIME

Check that each part of your speech is addressing one thought and only one thought. In the name of clarity, tease out bundles of ideas and deal with them one by one.

Vocabulary

The ill and unfit choice of words wonderfully obstructs the understanding.

Francis Bacon

Time spent labouring to find the correct word for the context is time well-spent. Settling for a word that is not quite right, or a phrase that says the same, but in ten words rather than one, is not good enough. Take the search for the right word seriously, and you will eventually produce a speech that is sharp and evocative. Take the lazy way out, and you will blunt the edge of your sword and 'wonderfully obstruct the understanding'.

In the same way, avoid using too many adjectives and adverbs. If you pick exactly the right nouns and verbs, you should not need to elaborate.

The importance of widening your normal vocabulary has already been mentioned in this and other sections. When writing, make use of a thesaurus, which will provide you with a host of alternatives for words that are overworked. Beware, however, of using words you do not understand. Take the time to look them up.

Guard against malapropisms – mistakenly using a word because it sounds similar to the correct word. For example, 'He was under the affluence of alcohol' or 'He was in hospital undergoing a prostrate operation'. While malapropisms are often hilarious, it is desirable to have your audience laugh with you, rather than at you.

Foreign words and phrases

The English language is one of the richest in the world. However, many people are tempted to pepper their speeches with foreign words and phrases. One of the differences between writing and speaking is that when listening to you speak, your audience is not able to refer to a dictionary whenever you use a term they do not understand. So, for the sake of audience understanding if nothing else, try to avoid this wherever possible.

Clichés and archaisms

Avoid clichés like the plague! Clichés are stereotyped phrases that are in constant use. They are generally overworked and consequently meaningless. Archaisms are old words that have long since passed out of common usage. They add nothing to a speech except unnecessary verbiage, and should also be avoided as far as possible.

PRACTICAL TECHNIQUES

Jargon, abbreviations and acronyms

The Collins English Dictionary defines jargon as: 1. specialized language concerned with a particular subject, culture or profession; 2. language characterized by pretentious vocabulary or meaning; 3. gibberish. Unless you are a specialist speaking to an audience of specialists, try to eradicate jargon from your speech, otherwise you run the risk of being misunderstood, thought pretentious or possibly even considered a total idiot. The same goes for uncommon abbreviations and acronyms.

Superlatives and hyperbole

Another element that should be avoided is exaggeration of any sort. Constant superlatives become wearing after a very short time, and like the boy who cried wolf, you will find your audience suitably sceptical when you come to describe something that is truly extraordinary. Keep your sense of proportion so that you have a wider range of imaginative contrast to call upon.

Using the first person singular

There is nothing wrong in speaking from your own experience. In fact, relating your own thoughts and emotions will do much to bring your speech onto a personal level. However, if you use only your own experience, you might be at risk of forgetting the audience's interest and needs. If a good speech identifies and speaks to the audience, this is the last thing you want to do. Repeated use of the word 'I' is a good indicator of this fault, and if you find it in your own speech, try harder to identify what you are saying with the experience of the audience.

Repeated use of the first person singular also tells the audience that you are self-absorbed, and, in extreme cases, it may show that you wish to take a group experience or success and make it your own. In this case, change 'I' into 'We', and you will not go far wrong (as long as you say who 'We' are).

BREAKING THE RULES

Most rules are made to be broken once in a while. As you improve with practise, you will begin to know when to break the rules. Stringing a line of clichés together, for example, or dropping a name with an air of wry self-mockery, could create a usefully humorous effect.

Using numbers

If it is difficult for a listener to grasp the words and phrases that go to form an argument, it is ten times more difficult for him or her to understand numbers on a first hearing.

Try to avoid quoting numbers as far as possible, and unless you need to be precise, always round numbers off and simplify them: 'about sixteen hundred' is much easier to understand than '1,674'; 'more than ten million' is a vast improvement on '10,065,124'. It is also useful to repeat numbers for emphasis and understanding.

When faced with percentages, try converting to a ratio or a fraction: '69.5% of the population' is almost the same as 'seven in ten people'; '33% of output' is 'nearly one-third'. More than 50% is a majority, and more than 80% could be said to be the vast majority. Less than 50% is a minority, and less than, say, 10% is a small minority.

If you are trying to convey the size, length or capacity of something, especially when it is very small or very large, a useful technique is to illustrate by comparison in terms that the audience will find familiar, for example:

- the length of so many buses parked nose-to-tail
- so many times the distance to the moon
- ten times smaller than a pin head
- a stretch of land three times the size of Wales
- a distance equivalent to twice around the world
- so high that it towers above St Paul's Cathedral

When tackling statistics, graphs, pie-charts or other forms of numerical information, always take time not only to cite the source and date, but also to interpret and draw conclusions:

[source and introduction] 'This graph, based on United Nations statistics, shows the number of visits to the cinema per head of population for five countries: the UK, Italy, France, the USA and Japan, between 1960 and 1990.'

[interpretation] 'You will see that the clear trend in all countries is down. In all countries, fewer visits were made in 1990 than in 1960.'

[interpretation] 'In 1990, the Americans went to the cinema the most often. The average American went to the movies four times in that year – roughly once every three months. That is double the rate for France, and four times the rate in Japan, who were the worst cinema-goers in 1990.'

[conclusion] 'While it seems, therefore, that cinema audiences are contracting all over the world, the best place for movie distribution is the USA.'

Using examples and illustrations
Audiences will find it easier to remember a good example than a bald fact. Examples also serve to reinforce and further illumin-

ate the argument. As often as possible, illustrate your points with lively anecdotes, examples and case studies. If you can find examples and illustrations that refer to the experience of your audience, then so much the better.

Using humour

The injunction always to try to entertain your audience does not mean that you should be aiming to provoke hysterical laughter at every turn. However, a little general humour can put an audience at its ease and add illustrative material to a speech.

Many people find it difficult to tell a joke successfully. They fear the joke falling flat and the resulting embarrassment for audience and speaker alike. If you feel uncomfortable with humour, do not feel that you have to use it.

If you would like to incorporate a few amusing anecdotes, witty one-liners or short jokes, never announce them as such. If you do the audience will be expecting to laugh, and the moment will be all the more excruciating if they don't.

Be careful of the targets of your humour. Avoid making sexist, racist or religious jokes that might offend members of the audience. The safest targets are yourself and common scapegoats, such as British Rail or politicians.

Despite the arrival of the so-called permissive society, don't allow yourself to become risqué in your humour. While you may succeed in raising a laugh, you may at the same time alienate your audience, and perhaps also lower the tone of the event at which you are speaking. Sleazy stories about naive honeymooners or venereal disease are, on the whole, best left to cabaret-circuit comedians.

Try to personalize your humour and to fit it to the occasion. Tell an anecdote as it if happened to you, or add the name of a member of the audience to a joke.

PRACTICAL TECHNIQUES

Unless you are very sure of your talents, don't try to relate jokes that rely on accents, and don't plan to do impersonations.

VET YOUR HUMOUR FOR:

- **bad taste**
- **offensiveness**
- **irrelevance**

Remarks in bad taste

There are many ways in which you might give offence to members of your audience, especially if you make jokes at their expense. Avoid, racism, sexism, bad language and slander (see pp.29–31 **General Research**). Other remarks in bad taste can include making fun of disadvantaged minorities (the disabled, for example), stereotyping followers of specific religions, or simply being inappropriate (levity at an occasion of solemnity, such as a funeral, for example). Always be aware of the spirit of the occasion, and tailor your language accordingly.

Name-dropping

Unless used in self-deprecating humour, name-dropping only irritates people. It is another temptation to resist.

Dynamics

Ensure that you vary the dynamics – the ebb and flow – of your speech. Rather than starting with the most important material, and allowing the content to drop away from that point onwards, spread the material evenly across the whole presentation. Look for grey areas that are relatively uninteresting, and bolster them with sparky anecdotes or more thought-provoking evidence.

Within each section of the body of the speech, present the less interesting material first and work up to a crescendo, before linking to the next section.

If you expect a reaction from the audience, or if you have just made a splash with some outrageous statement, and you would like to leave time for it to sink in, write in a pause. Use a line of dots to remind yourself.

Adding dynamics of this nature ensures that there is variety and even content, giving the audience something worth listening to from start to finish.

Checking for faults

When you have finished drafting your speech, put it to one side for a while – overnight is long enough. When you return to your desk, look at the notes you made on the audience (its needs and expectations), your objectives, the occasion and venue and your topic. Re-read your speech with your thoughts on these subjects in your mind, answering the questions on the following checklist:

- Does the opening make a suitable splash?
- Is the topic clearly defined?
- Have you presented the audience with your credentials?
- Have you appealed to their needs throughout the speech, especially at bridging points?
- Does your argument follow a logical order, step by step?
- Have you made use of repetition and linking passages?
- Is there anything that is superfluous and should be removed?
- Is the close strong?
- Is your speech relevant to the occasion?
- Is the language you have used suitable for the level of the audience?

PRACTICAL TECHNIQUES

- Have you included interesting illustrations to back up as many of your points as possible?
- Have you eradicated: jargon, exaggeration; name-dropping; clichés; and moments of bad taste?
- Have you spread your material evenly across the entire speech?
- IS THIS SPEECH GOING TO ENABLE YOU TO ACHIEVE YOUR OBJECTIVES?

KEY POINTS

√ your speech is a conversation
√ be yourself
√ keep it simple
√ avoid:
malapropisms
clichés and archaisms
foreign words and phrases
jargon, abbreviations and acronyms
first person singular
superlatives and hyperbole
remarks in bad taste
name-dropping
√ handle with care:
new vocabulary
numbers
examples and illustrations
humour
check your speech for style faults

VISUAL AIDS

Visual aids – from photocopied handouts to professionally-produced audio-visual presentations – can add a second dimension to a verbal presentation. Of course, they are not suitable for all occasions – they would almost certainly be out of place accompanying an after-dinner speech or when toasting the bridesmaids at a wedding. Visual aids are most useful when lecturing, addressing conferences or giving presentations in a business context.

Appropriate use of visual aids

The amount of time, effort and money you decide to devote to visual aids depends on the occasion. Promotional presentations in a business context may demand computer-generated graphics and professionally-printed, full-colour brochures or handouts. Informal meetings or lectures may only call for a flip-chart or a few well-chosen slides. Always consider the cost of the visual you decide to use, and find out who (if not you) is going to pay for it.

Correct use of a well-considered visual aid can save time otherwise given over to lengthy explanations, add interest and help audience retention of facts. However, confused, gratuitous or badly-presented visual aids can become a positive hindrance.

When you have planned your speech – perhaps you have written it out in full as suggested in the section **Planning and Writing** – consider whether it would be appropriate to introduce a visual aid. This section gives some advice on when and how to use visual aids, and lists some of the advantages and disadvantages of each type. Notes of presenting visual aids appear in the section on **Successful Delivery** (pp.90–91).

Visual aids – uses and abuses

The human brain is much more receptive to visual stimulus than speech. As a consequence, information presented visually is more easily understood and remembered than information presented orally. When you next walk into a room where the television is on, notice that the eyes of most people in the room are drawn towards the screen, even if they are listening to what you are saying, and even if the sound of the television is turned off. In the same way, a visual aid will draw the audience's attention away from any other kind of stimulus, including the sound of your voice.

In the battle for your audience's attention, then, a visual aid will always win. Therefore, it is vital to ensure that speech and visuals do not compete with one another. Make sure that you use visuals only to illustrate – never to make a point. Always give less information on a graphic that you are presenting at the same time orally, and never assume that a visual will speak for itself – always draw a conclusion to reduce the chances of the audience misinterpreting the visual.

Visual aids should only be used in the following circumstances:

- To clarify complex ideas and information (such as figures and statistics).
- To demonstrate the workings of a machine or process.
- To emphasize a point.
- To illustrate a point.
- To summarize an argument.

Do not allow a visual aid to carry the burden of the argument. In the same way, never design a visual aid that gives a list of headings, telling the audience the content of your speech before you start. This is patronizing (audiences are quite capable of following your speech if you have constructed it well enough), and it can ruin the element of surprise. When confronted with a visual of this type, members of the audience are likely to run through the headings in their minds, decide what you are likely to say about each, and come to their own conclusions, all before you have even drawn your first introductory breath! By doing this, you have also lost control of the audience's thought process. You have allowed your travelling companions to run off into the middle distance rather than keeping them with you and leading them step by step along the right path.

It is, however, useful to give a list of headings as you summarize your argument – you have at that stage already said most of what you want them to hear, and the visual will lodge it more firmly in their memories.

Hints for good graphics

When creating graphics for visual aids, use as few words as possible. The written word will compete more than any other graphic with your spoken word. Limit the use of words in graphics to labels (identifying parts of a machine, for example) and summaries. Always write out words horizontally – even when labelling the vertical axis of a graph or a section of a pie chart.

Pie charts and graphs are good ways of representing proportions and percentages, and trends. It is a good idea to avoid using tables of figures – they are difficult to see and usually give too much information. Most tables can be reduced to a simple graph. However, if you cannot find any other way of illustrating a point that demands to be clarified, emphasize the important figures using different colours.

If you think a graph may be too boring to look at, consider using icons to represent the concept embodied in the figures. For example, if your company sells books you could redraw a bar graph showing increasing sales as ever-growing piles of books. If your information compares numbers of people engaged in different leisure-time activities, use simple icons representing each activity: golf clubs for golf, a plant in a pot or a spade for gardening, a needle and thread for embroidery.

When creating graphics in this way, make sure that the number of icons you use corresponds to the figures you want to present. For example, one million people might be represented by one stick person, six million people by six, and so on.

Flow charts can be used as an alternative to a list to enumerate the stages in a process. They have the added advantage that you can link stages or make connections between ideas using lines or arrows.

Colour can be used to great effect when creating graphics. It can add interest, differentiate between different points, or between sections of your presentation, and emphasize important information. Choose colours that contrast, and try to use strong shades – pastel colours are difficult to read, and give a wishy-washy effect. Some colours have specific meanings, which you may need to keep in mind: for instance, red is usually a warning, and green means go. Also, some colour combinations are not visible enough for use in large venues, for instance blue on green, white on yellow and pink on red.

Keep your visuals looking uniform – any changes in style distract the audience's attention. If you are using handwritten transparencies for an overhead projector, do not slip in one or two that have been typeset using a computer. If you are using several colours, use one colour for one concept or train of thought, and another colour for the next. Make sure that all your graphics are of the same size, and make sure that the size is visible from the back of the venue, and by all members of the audience.

If your handwriting is poor, it is better to have visuals written by an artist or to have them typeset. If you think your handwriting is clear enough, it is still wise to stick to capital letters for clarity.

Visual aids are fun to create, and they can spice up any presentation. However, don't let your creative urges run away with you. Check for simplicity and relevance. Never use too many different types of aid. Jumping about from one piece of equipment to another makes you look more like a conjuring act than a speaker, and the more visual aids you employ the greater the chances of disaster.

Focus on visual aids

There are several different types of visual aid that can be used to illustrate your presentation:

● **flip chart**
A large pad of paper mounted on an easel. The sheets of paper can be flipped backwards and forwards, or torn off and discarded. Flip charts can be pre-prepared with graphics and used simply for illustration, or they can be used as a jotting pad, to note down contributions from the audience during brainstorming sessions, or for emphasis. Flip charts are best used with informal groups of fewer that about 20 people.

● **paste boards**
A series of stiff pieces of card that can be propped up on an easel, paste boards can be used in a similar way to flip charts, with small informal groups. They can be pre-prepared to a high standard, and you can pack them up in a portfolio after the presentation to be used again some other time.

● **blackboard/whiteboard**
Can be used in much the same way as a flip chart, to make notes or to add emphasis in a fairly intimate, informal context.

PRACTICAL TECHNIQUES

• overhead projector

The graphics are created using felt-tip pens on sheets or continuous rolls of acetate, and then projected onto a large screen. Overhead projectors can therefore be used with a slightly larger audience than flip charts or paste boards. They can be used to demonstrate an idea, or for presenting graphics, pie charts and flow charts. The overhead projector enables you to present the information at the same time as facing the audience, and you can also write as you go, underlining for emphasis, for example. By using an accessory called an episcope, you can also present non-transparent materials, such as press cuttings and photographs. Remember, though, that to do this you will need to dim the lights in the room.

• handouts

Written information given to each member of the audience. Handouts should only be used if you want to supply a large amount of extra information (perhaps full of figures, as in company accounts or sales figures) or if you want to stop your audience taking notes. They could conceivably also be used as back-up if you are suspicious that the other visual equipment at the venue is likely to go wrong! Always proofread your handout before you have it duplicated. Resist the temptation to give the audience a résumé of what you are going to say – they might then decide to read your speech in the comfort of their own homes. Give some thought to when you are going to let your audience have the handouts. Passing them around as you are speaking will distract the audience's attention. Unless you need to refer the audience to particular items on the handout, the best time to distribute is at the end of your presentation – but let the audience know that they are getting one, and that they therefore need not take notes.

• slides

35 mm slides are a very versatile visual aid. They can be used to present graphics, to demonstrate how something works, to show maps or straight photographs – landscapes, people, places, objects, etc. Bear in mind though that slide shows take a great deal of preparation. Unless you are planning to operate the slide projector yourself, you will need to produce a clearly annotated script for the slide projectionist. In any case, you should note down the places where you intend to change the slide, and give yourself some indication of what should be on the screen at any given time so that you are certain that you have not slipped up. (Many lecture halls are equipped with lecterns that have mirrors attached so that you can check what is on the screen without turning your back on the audience.) Don't plan to use too many slides, and leave them on the screen long enough for you to explain and the audience to digest their contents. It is sometimes possible to synchronize two projectors to improve the flow from one slide to the next. (But resist the temptation to use double the number of slides!)

If there are parts of your speech that will not require a slide on the screen, don't plan to turn the projector off or to leave the screen empty. Instead, prepare a neutral slide to fill the gap – perhaps a general picture or a coloured background showing your company's logo. One disadvantage of a slide projector is that once you have selected and ordered your slides, it is very difficult to skip passages or to change the order. Consider whether this might be a problem in the speaking situation you are planning.

• scale models and other exhibits

The presence of strange or interesting objects can arouse the curiosity of an audience – it can also distract attention. They can be used to demonstrate the workings of machines, or simply as

PRACTICAL TECHNIQUES

exhibits. Decide when the audience is to get its first sight of your exhibit. If you are to avoid distracting speculation, perhaps you should keep it completely out of sight until you are ready to use it.

● **audio-visual presentations**
Presentations that include recorded narration or music as well as images can easily look amateurish. If you are considering putting together a film of this kind, it is best to consult a professional production company.

When deciding whether to make use of a visual aid, and what kind of aid to use, take into consideration the size and layout of the venue, the size of the audience, and the purpose for which you need the aid. Annotate the full script of your speech with notes on the visual aids you plan to use, and write down what you intend to say about them.

Incompetent use of visual aids can lead to total disaster, so make sure that you really do need them before you go ahead. Follow the suggestions in the section on **Successful Delivery** (pp.90–91) for presentation of visual aids.

KEY POINTS

√ use visual aids to illustrate, clarify and add interest
√ choose the visual aid that fits your needs
√ ensure that your visual aids support rather than compete with the spoken word
√ keep it simple
√ don't use too many different aids.

SUCCESSFUL DELIVERY

Few audiences see, or even think about, the amount of work that a speaker puts in to prepare a speech. Fairly or not, they judge the person on the podium by their performance on the day.

Good delivery is a matter of being confident that you can remember what to say, and when and how you want to say it. It is also about communicating with an audience, not only through what you say, but through the attitude of your body, and by the expression in your voice. Good delivery, like a good speaking style, can be learned through adequate rehearsal and control of your nerves.

Presenting a speech

There are several ways in which to present a speech that you have prepared. Some formal conference occasions, for example, demand that you read your paper verbatim. Even if the form does not demand that the speaker reads the speech, you may decide that you must do so in order to survive the ordeal. Most speakers, however, prefer to forego the security of reading, and rely on some form of memory-jogging notes to keep them on track. The advantage in doing so is that in this way they are more able to communicate with the audience.

Memorizing your speech

Some people have very good memories, and if you are one of them, you may come to the conclusion that the best way to deliver your talk is to learn it by heart. This is probably one of the worst things a speaker can do. If a speech is a kind of conversation, then it must be allowed to flow in as natural and spontaneous a manner as possible. Learning a script by heart means that its words are fixed in the brain. Because of this, the speaker will find it exceptionally difficult to step away from it on the spur of the moment to add a new phrase here, an impromptu anecdote there, to inject the spontaneity vital to communicating with the audience.

Watch people who are reciting from memory. Their energy and attention is turned inwards, rather than reaching out towards the audience. If you are trying to remember what comes next, you are not going to de directing all your energies into communication. Watch people who are trying to remember something – they normally look up and to the right, rather than directly at the person they are talking to. The only people capable of delivering – communicating – a memorized speech to an audience are actors, who have spent many years in specialized training.

Apart from the problem of communicating with the audience, memorizing your speech depends, sometimes fatally, on a skill that is fallible. Speakers have been known to lose their way in the heat of the moment, or to dry up completely. Without someone else beside you to prompt you, this could spell disaster.

By all means, imprint the important parts of your talk onto your memory – the opening sentence, perhaps, or the linking passages. But, however good your memory, it would pay to consider one of the alternative methods of delivery detailed below.

Reading your speech

The first thing to be said about this method of presenting a speech is that, like memorizing your speech, it will decrease the spontaneity of the performance. The speaker becomes tied to the words on the page and therefore is less inclined to ad lib. As a result, the presentation is at risk of becoming stale and unnatural. Reading from a script also reduces the opportunity you have to make eye contact with the audience, and to register their reaction to what you are saying (see pp.78–79).

Having said this, there are two circumstances when it may be necessary to read from a script. First, you may be addressing an academic conference, where it is mandatory to read the paper that has been submitted to an audience. Second, you may be involved in a complex audio-visual presentation involving one or more technicians (projectionists, tape-operators, etc.). In this case, you will need to have annotated the script with cues for the audio-visual elements, and it is important for smooth co-ordination that you stick to it.

In the first case, the language employed to write the paper is likely to be fairly formal, constrained as you are by the expert needs of the academic audience. You can add some interest to your personal presentations by including short anecdotes or illustrations that were not used in the original paper. If, however, you are constrained merely by the need to co-ordinate your words with other elements in the presentation, try to make the script as conversational as possible. Notes on a conversational style are given in the section on **Improving Your Style** (p.48).

If you do intend to read from a script, it may be a good idea to have it typed on a word processor that can generate larger-than-normal type. Make sure that it is double-spaced, and that you do not have to turn over a page in mid-sentence. Start each new stage of your argument on a new page so that you can take advantage of the natural pause to turn the page. Make sure that you number the pages (imagine yourself dropping your script as you mount the podium!) and try to use firm rather than flimsy paper, a constantly wilting script can be distracting to the audience. It may also be a good idea to fix the script into a ring binder. This not only looks more professional, it also enables you to turn the pages without fumbling.

PRACTICAL TECHNIQUES

A third circumstance in which you might find yourself 'reading' from a prepared verbatim script is if you are giving a political speech or a business speech that may attract publicity. The practise of using a full script in these circumstances may be due to the fact that many speeches of this type are written, not by the speaker, but by professional speech-writers. Often too, the form of words has been designed to be quotable, or written in such a way as to not be misconstrued.

To avoid such a presentation turning into something more akin to reading a statement than delivering a speech, make sure that you have time to rehearse fully. As you rehearse, mark out the key thought in the speech, and punctuate the text with reminders to yourself to pause for better effect. Try to become so familiar with the speech that all you need to do is glance down every time you come to a new point, to keep yourself on track. When you look at the script, don't read the headings, a glance should be enough to remind you where you are. With adequate rehearsal, you will find yourself conversant enough with the words you need to get out to satisfy your speech-writer or publicity aides, but you will also be free enough to inject a feeling of spontaneity into your delivery.

Delivering a speech from a full script may be a requirement thrust upon you by circumstance, or, if you are inexperienced, you may feel the need for the full script as a fail-safe against serious bouts of nerves. However, if communication is the watchword in good delivery, by far the best way to present a speech is to take your courage in your hands and determine to work from notes.

Abbreviating your script

The most effective method of delivering a speech of almost any kind is to abbreviate the full-length script to a series of key words that serve to jog the memory as the talk progresses. These words can be written on a sheet of paper or on a series of blank postcards or index cards that can be more easily held in the shaking hand.

The advantage of this system is that because you are not being spoon-fed with the actual words of your script, you are free to extemporize, to go in search of fresh words and phrases. Because you are only reading key words rather than complete sentences, your eyes are free to roam the room, making eye contact with members of the audience, and you are more likely to pick up more of their attitude to what you are saying. You may also be able to skip sections if time is running short, or shuffle arguments at the last minute in the light of what other speakers have said.

Physically, cue cards or crib sheets are much less unwieldy than a full script. As a consequence you may not need a lectern or desk on which to rest your material, and so you can do away with the physical barrier between your body and the audience. The effect of this is to signal to the audience that you are relaxed, and that you want to be closer to them. You also have your hands, arms and upper body free to give expression to your words, a very powerful tool with which to improve your communication with the audience.

ROOM FOR MANOEUVRE

Whatever method you decide to use in delivering your speech, make sure that you leave some space to make notes. You may want to reply to a previous speaker, or to note down an impromptu thought. Place a blank card in your pack, or type your crib sheet or full script with especially wide margins so that you have space to do this.

PRACTICAL TECHNIQUES

Most of all, working from brief notes allows you the freedom to think on your feet, while giving you the security of knowing that, if you lose your way, you have only to glance down to find your way back to the right path.

If you have followed the process for putting together a speech that has been described in this book, you will now have a full script in front of you. Work through the script and underline or circle the key ideas. Mark out also the opening sentences, the linking passages, the appeals and the closing remarks. Begin to rehearse the speech using the full script and the annotations you have added (see pp.91–96 on rehearsals). When you come to the point where you are happy with the substance of the argument, start to make the notes from which you will deliver the speech.

Write onto the cue cards (or crib sheet) each of the annotated elements in order. Apart from the opening and close, the links and appeals, write down only key words to cover each heading and each sub-heading. Write each point on a different card. Include one-word memory-joggers to cue the use of visual aids. Do not write too small, and do not cover the cards or sheet with

---

QUOTATIONS

When writing notes for cue cards or crib sheets, make sure that you write down quotations in full – it is important that you quote accurately.

---

notes – you will find them very difficult to read. Try to use as few words as possible. As with the full script, make sure that you number the sheets in the correct running order.

If you have opted not to write out a full script, you should have some form of plan from which to work, and provided you have thought out your entire speech from start to finish, you should be able to make effective memory-joggers. Do not try to use your original plan as a crib sheet. Your speech should have evolved significantly since you jotted down your first ideas, and besides, making a new plan at this stage will considerably aid you when it comes to remembering what you have to say.

If you are using a crib sheet rather than cards, it is useful to mark out the different elements of the speech in different colours. Red for the opening, blue for section headings, green for sub-headings, and so on. This will help you to remember where you are in your speech.

Some speakers rely on their visual aids to act as memory-joggers. Write key words in pencil on the side of a flip chart, or note them down in the margins of overhead-projector transparencies.

SCISSOR SECTIONS

As you are making your notes and rehearsing with them, mark out sections of your speech that could be cut if you find you are running over time, or if your time limit is cut for some reason. This will enable you to adjust quickly and without panic to what is often a last-minute change.

Obviously the only way that crib sheets or cue cards are going to work on the day is by practising with them. Follow the guidelines on pp.68–70 to ensure that you become confident in their use, and that the technique you have chosen really does do the job. Becoming adept at using notes to carry you through, or at enlivening a script read verbatim, is only one third of the art of successful delivery. Control of one's visual appearance and of one's voice are the other two thirds.

In person

Human methods of communication do not rely solely on words. People watch each other constantly for physical clues as to what people are thinking and feeling, as to who they are, and where in society they belong. Equally, the human brain takes in a great deal of information about a person's verbal message from his or her tone of voice. Unlike the Chinese languages, inflexions in English and other European languages are not essential to meaning, but expression – pitch, pace and volume – provides a clue to the relative importance of heard information. It is important, therefore, to take control, not only of the material you want to put across, but also of the signals your body and voice give to the audience.

Taking control of these two methods of communication does not necessarily mean presenting a fake persona. This is the last

---

BODY LANGUAGE

In the speaking situation, body language can be divided into:
- **dress**
- **posture and body movement**
- **eye contact**
- **hand gestures**
- **facial expression**

---

thing you should try to do – as in the words you choose, you must also strive to be natural in your physical presentation. What it does mean is taking advantage of their power to convey your message. In order to do this, you must be fully conversant with the material you have produced for the occasion, and you must be able to put it across with energy, enthusiasm and confidence.

First impressions

When you first move into a person's field of vision, they make an instant judgement on your appearance. They immediately take in some very minute details which tell them about who and what you are. The same thing happens when you first appear in front of your audience. The style of your dress will tell them first and foremost whether you are one of them, or whether you are part of a different social group. This kind of 'tribal recognition' (one of us or one of them) happens in almost all situations. A person who is perceived by their dress to be one of the tribe is likely to be better received than one who is patently from another, who may be received at least with caution. A person who is 'one of us' is much more likely to understand our needs and concerns, and therefore to say something of interest to us, than 'one of them'.

Added to this is the fact that people who dress smartly, and who pay attention to their appearance, are perceived as being more authoritative than those who are slovenly. The thinking goes that a person who sets no great importance by their dress is equally casual in their thinking, and may well have little of worth to say. Equally, if you look good, you feel good. If you look smart, you think smart. If it seems to your audience that you have just fallen out of bed perhaps your brain is still asleep.

Take advantage of these common perceptions, to put you and your audience in the right frame of mind to present and listen to your talk with enthusiasm and attention. Dress in a smart, but conservative way. Avoid wearing anything that is too outlandish – you will alienate most audiences (drawing attention to the fact that you are not 'one of them'), and you will probably distract their attention from what you are saying. However, avoid play-acting. Do not go so far that your appearance belies your personality. Pay attention to detail: clean your shoes, replace missing shirt buttons, wear ladder-free stockings. Every part of your dress will be on display, and the audience will miss nothing.

Having said all that, do not overdress. Invest a little time in working out what looks right for the occasion. Call the organizers and find out what the form is (especially if the occasion may require formal dress of some sort).

Aim to be appropriate, and let nothing distract attention from your material.

> **A man's body and his mind ... are exactly like a jerkin and a jerkin's lining; – rumple the one, – you rumple the other.**
> **Lawrence Sterne, *Tristram Shandy***

Posture and movement
The second element of your appearance that an audience will detect at first sight is your posture, and the way you move. As with many animals, our posture and movement sends some very strong signals about our attitude to the situation that we are in, and to the people we are with. Stooping and bowing the head indicates that we are unsure of our ground, whereas a head held high signals confidence.

From the moment you see the audience for the first time, pay as much attention as you can to your posture and movement. Hold your shoulders square, keep you head up and avoid slouching. Sit towards the front of the chair, rather than leaning back. Whether you are a man or a woman, it is better not to cross your legs at the knee. If you have to, cross them at the ankle to the side. Do not let your rib cage sag downwards. Hold it so that your spine is straight, rather than bowed out. Try to convey the impression that you are relaxed yet alert.

When you rise to talk (and always speak on your feet, even if you are addressing an informal departmental meeting), do so with purpose. If you have to move from your seat to your speaking position (a lectern, perhaps, or the front of the room), fix your eyes on the place you want to get to, and move directly to it. Even if your heart is pumping and you have a lump of terror in your throat, move as if you cannot wait to start speaking, but without rushing.

When you are speaking, stand upright. Try not to hold onto the nearest available object for balance. Place your feet a few inches apart, with the weight on the balls rather than the heels of your feet. This means that your body is balanced, and also that you are leaning towards the audience slightly. Do not rock backwards and forwards. Plant your feet firmly on the floor, and stay there. Hold your upper body upright so that your lungs can get a good breath of air. Putting one hand in a pocket conveys a relaxed and informal message, but hands in pockets encourages your rib cage to cave inwards, so that you are unable to take in enough breath to project your words, and you look slovenly.

From this basic speaking position, you should be able to move freely and in a relaxed but purposeful manner. Avoid shuffling around. If you want to change your position, do it during a link, to reinforce the transition from one idea to another. Alternatively, you could take a step towards the audience to emphasize a point. In any event, try not to do it too often – every movement of your whole body should add something to the meaning of the words.

Eye contact

Turn on the television. Watch an actor who is clearly telling a lie, or who does not want to divulge a secret. What is he doing with his eyes? In nine cases out of ten, the actor is doing his level best to avoid looking directly into the eyes of the other person.

By making eye contact, we are expressing our openness towards other people. We are also showing that we are not frightened of them and that we are interested in their thoughts, feelings and reactions. When eye contact is made, the listener's attention is grabbed, and a direct line of communication is set up. Making eye contact with members of the audience is one of the most valuable skills a speaker can learn.

Eye contact can be practised in almost any social situation, and you will be surprised how it changes people's reaction to you. They will become more attentive, and they will be more willing to trust what you say. They will begin to look upon you as a more approachable person – exactly the kind of responses you would ideally like to elicit from your audience.

When you are speaking to a group, avoid picking out a single person in the audience and making eye contact exclusively with him or her. This will make the individual you choose very uncomfortable indeed, and the rest of the audience will begin to feel excluded! Instead, make eye contact with different individuals around the room, so that you take in the whole audience.

If you are inexperienced, and extremely nervous, you may not wish to make eye contact straight away. In this case, deliver your first couple of lines to a point slightly above the audience's head, somewhere in the middle distance. (Do not fix your eyes on an object, or you may find members of the audience turning round to see what it is that interests you so much.) However, as soon as you come to your first appeal (see **Planning and Writing** p.37), take the opportunity to start making eye contact.

You will find that if you have opted to read your speech from a script, you will find it very difficult to find time to make eye contact. It cannot be emphasized enough that eye contact is central to delivering your message in a personal and potent way, and for this reason it is important to find ways to free your eyes from the written word. If you cannot master the art of making eye contact with the people to whom you are speaking, you may well find that your speech-making efforts are doomed to failure.

Hand gestures

As with body movement, gestures of the hands and arms should add to, rather than distract from, the spoken word. They should be produced as part of your enthusiasm for and knowledge of your subject.

FOREIGN GESTURES

If you are speaking to a foreign audience, be very careful of the hand gestures that you make. Different cultures sometimes assign different meanings to gestures, and you may find that a gesture that is innocuous to Europeans may be outrageously obscene to Arabs.

Gesture in a way that improves your audience's understanding of the words you are saying, or for emphasis. Watch how other people make use of gesture in everyday conversations. Notice how some gestures (such as pointing with a stabbing

79

motion at the listener, or clenching and raising the fist) are much stronger than others. Gestures have very specific meanings: counting on the fingers can be useful if you are enumerating a list; holding the hand outstretched with the palm upwards indicates that you have something you wish to offer the audience – a thought, perhaps; you can divide a subject into two sections by moving the hands apart from each other; or you can reject an idea by holding the hand up with the palm towards the audience.

There are two things to avoid when it comes to hand gestures. First, beware of fidgeting. Many people have little habits that they do not notice themselves, but which can cause irritation and even hilarity among the audience. But they also betray nervousness. Some people scratch their noses or stroke their beards. They play anxiously with rings, or pull their ear lobes. Worse still, some people have a habit of covering up their mouth with a hand. At the later stages of rehearsal, ask a good friend to watch

In a few cases, twitches or tics are the result of a nervous disorder, and those who suffer from them are unable to do anything about them. If you are afflicted with this problem, it may be worthwhile to draw attention to the fact early on in your speech, and explain the reason for it. By doing so, you have answered the audience's most immediate question, and with luck they will put it into the backs of their minds and get on with the real business of the day – listening to what you have to say.

you as you deliver your speech. Ask him or her to watch for these mannerisms, and to shout out if they spot you fidgeting.

Second, try not to make too many meaningless gestures. Stick to hand movements that mean something, that enable the audience to understand your thought processes more clearly. If your friend tells you that your hands are moving too much, try delivering your speech without any gestures at all. This should tell you when you really need to move your hands, and when to keep them still.

When you are not using your hands, it is often difficult to know what to do with them. Cue cards or a crib sheet could come in handy here. Hold your notes with one hand at about waist level. Your other hand is then free to gesture, and it should hang quietly by your side when not in use. If you are using a lectern, you may rest one hand (not both, and never lean on your forearms) to the side of your notes. Alternatively, simply allow both hands to hang by your sides. This may feel unnatural to you, and you may have to practise, but it certainly looks relaxed, open and neutral.

There are any number of hand gestures you can use, and if you study to use them naturally, you will find that your communications armoury is greatly enhanced.

Facial expression

The golden rule on facial expression is: smile, but not too much. A smile means that you are friendly, that you are happy to be there, and that you are glad of the opportunity to relate your thoughts to the audience. An open smile will relax both you and your audience – practise it along with your speech.

However, if you smile fixedly through thick and thin, and allow no other response to register on your face, people will begin to mistrust you – it gives the impression that you are hiding something.

If you are trying to hide anything from your audience, it is probably fear. This may manifest itself on your face if not as a smile, then as a frown or an impassive poker face. Avoid both: frowning can be construed as anger or aggression, and a poker face, like the fixed smile, can be hiding something. True enthusiasm for the subject, coupled with good voice control, should animate your face, and if you allow yourself to be animated (in a controlled way) you will not have to use your face to mask your nerves.

THE KEY VISUAL ELEMENTS ARE:

- **enthusiasm**
- **vitality**
- **alertness**
- **naturalness**

Rehearse until hand gestures and body movements are second nature – a seamless part of the meaning you wish to convey. Your appearance will be a powerful weapon against audience indifference.

Voice control

The third element in delivering a speech is your voice. Good vocal delivery can be broken down into two factors: volume – speaking to be heard; and expression – speaking to be understood. The basic skill in voice control is breathing.

The noise made by the human voice comes from the vibration

of air on the vocal cords, located in the throat. As with all wind instruments, the force of the air passing over the cords determine the volume of the sound produced. In public speaking, it is useful to have a solid column of air with which to 'sound' longer than normal phrases at the right volume.

The most important muscle as far as breathing is concerned is the diaphragm. It is located in the upper body just below the rib cage, and when it is relaxed, it forms an arch shape. When the diaphragm is taut, it flattens out, pushing the organs of the lower body outwards, and expanding the volume of the lungs. This causes a vacuum in the lungs, into which air is drawn through the nose or mouth. As the diaphragm relaxes again, the air is pushed out. Control of the diaphragm, therefore, enables you to control the column of air that you use to make sounds.

The best position for you to be in for good breath control is standing upright, but if you are forced to sit, make sure that your back is upright, to give your lungs space to expand.

There are many breathing exercises that you can do to improve your ability to control your diaphragm. Here is one that is simple and not too strenuous.

● Stand upright with your feet a few inches apart, and hands hanging by your sides. Be relaxed.

● Take a deep breath through your nose, mentally counting slowly to four. Notice how the diaphragm flattens out, and how it causes your belly to protrude slightly. Do not lift your shoulders, this has the reverse effect of reducing the amount of space in the lungs.

● Hold the breath in your lungs to a count of four. Notice how, when you are holding the breath in the lungs, the diaphragm is in the flat position.

PRACTICAL TECHNIQUES

● Gently allow the air to come out through your mouth to a count of eight. Consciously control your diaphragm so that it returns to its relaxed arched position without 'snapping back'. Repeat the exercise a couple of times.

You should try to make your upper body as relaxed as possible during this exercise. Deep, controlled breathing in this way not only provides you with a solid column of air with which to sound the vocal cords, but it also helps to calm the nerves and relieve tension.

If you find that your head is beginning to swim, it is because you are allowing an unaccustomed amount of oxygen into your brain. Try to avoid this feeling. The remedy is to revert to your usual shallow breathing, and perhaps you might like to sit down.

It is a good idea to try making a sound when doing this exercise:

● Take in the air, and when you are holding it, open your mouth to say 'ahh'. At this stage, do not allow any air out of your lungs.

● After the count of four, slowly relax the diaphragm, maintaining the tone and volume of the sound. Count to eight. Try to judge the amount of air you have in your lungs so that at the end of the eight, you do not have to take a quick breath, or expel any air left in the lungs. The whole exercise should be relaxed and gentle.

There is no mystery about breath control. It is simply a matter of being aware of what your diaphragm is doing, and of knowing that you can consciously control its movement to produce your words. Once you are able to do this, you have the basic skill with which to control the volume and tone of your voice.

Volume

Have you ever been at a gathering – a reception or a cocktail party – where people are standing in groups talking to one another? Suddenly, above the gentle hum of conversation, one person's voice rings out. Other conversations stop as everybody turns to find out where the voice is coming from and what it is saying. It is considered a faux pas to draw attention to yourself in this way at a social function. However, one of the necessities of speaking in public is that you do just this.

Some people think that because they are speaking in public they need to shout. This is not the case. If you are speaking in a room where you need to shout to be heard at the back, you should perhaps be using a microphone. Aim to speak only slightly louder than you would in everyday conversation. In most instances it is not necessary to declaim your speech – you are not a priest proclaiming the words of the communion service.

Open your mouth wider than you would normally. Do not distort your face, simply allow space for the sound to escape. Set the volume of your voice just one notch higher than normal, and you will find that you are able to maintain a conversational feel, while still being heard. Take a good lungful of air, and stay in control of your diaphragm, and with practise, a suitable volume will come to you as second nature.

Expression

The way a speaker expresses his or her words adds to their meaning much in the same way as hand gestures. Expression involves three elements: pitch variation – the tone of your voice; pace – the speed at which you speak; and phrasing – sculpting your phrases into a meaningful form. Rehearsal with a tape recorder (see p.93) should enable you to pinpoint faults in your expression.

PRACTICAL TECHNIQUES

TALKING TO YOURSELF

If you are not used to speaking in public, get used to the sound of your own voice. Read to your children, or get into the habit of reading the newspaper aloud. If you have time, and the interest, find a book of famous speeches and read them aloud. You may find it useful to mark them up for expression before you start.

Pitch

As a rule, young people tend to have higher pitched voices than older people. It follows that because older people are considered to have more authority than younger people, those with lower voices are thought of in the same way. Also, the pitch of a person's voice varies, depending on what kind of emotional state they are in. A high tone indicates nervousness, whereas a low tone shows that a person is calm and in control.

Some teachers of public speaking advocate that you work to lower the tone of your voice for just these reasons. However, if one of the keys to good delivery is being natural, this may not be a good idea. If you consider yourself to be one of those rare unfortunate people who is cursed with a truly painful speaking voice, a voice that makes people wince every time you open your mouth, then perhaps you should seek the services of a voice trainer. For the vast majority of people, however, controlled breathing, along with slow speaking and careful phrasing should automatically improve the tone of your voice.

Pace

Slow down. You must give your audience time to hear and assimilate the words you are saying, and yourself time to think about where the next sentence is coming from. Slower than normal speech also indicates that you have something of importance to say.

As you work with your speech, add indications of pauses of different lengths. These are not five-second 'pregnant' pauses, simply moments with which to punctuate your speech pattern for better understanding. Pause before and after important sentences. Pause before you start a linking passage. Pause before and after appeals. Use the time to make eye contact with the audience.

Apart from generally speaking more slowly than normal, conscious use of changes in pace can stimulate the audience's interest at moments when you perceive it is beginning to flag. (Incidentally, raising or lowering the volume of your voice slightly has the same effect – notice how on commercial television, the adverts are louder than the film you were just watching, a policy intended to catch the attention of viewers.) Explanations of terms or concepts should be slowed down, whereas link passages could be speeded up to a brisker pace in order to gently shove yourself and the audience from one section to the next.

Slowing your speech should also give you time to improve your diction. It is not necessary to affect a 'received pronunciation' (RP) accent, but do make sure that you do not swallow your words. It is only a matter of opening your mouth slightly wider than normal, and working your jaw a little more energetically.

Phrasing

The words you have written out in a full script fall into small groups – perhaps sentences or parts of sentences (individual

PRACTICAL TECHNIQUES

clauses). To better communicate the meaning of each of these groups of words, you need to take each one as an individual unit and try to imbue it with the single meaning that it contains.

Different meanings require different 'shapes'. A question, for example, should be spoken with an upturn at the end. Without the upturn, the question could be misunderstood as a statement. In rehearsal, sculpt each phrase according to its meaning. Do

---

VOICE CONTROL – DOS AND DON'TS

- Do speak slowly.
- Don't shout.
- Do make sure that you can be understood.
- Do keep control of your breathing.
- Don't allow your voice to dip downwards at the end of sentences – keep it on a level unless you are asking a question.
- Don't over-dramatize.
- Don't strain your voice – relax and enjoy yourself.
- Don't distort your face.
- Don't breathe so deeply that your head starts to swim.
- Do practise varying the volume, pace and expression in your voice.
- Don't eat too much before you deliver your speech – the contents of your stomach will hinder the expansion of your lungs.
- Don't smoke too much – smoking irritates the throat and reduces your lung capacity.

---

not over-dramatize, simply speak slowly, to give yourself time to think about and craft the meaning you wish to express.

Using a microphone

In general, forswear the use of a microphone – it can make the voice sound unnatural and hinders the task of appearing to be conversational. However, there are some circumstances when using a microphone is unavoidable: at open air meetings (fetes, political rallies, for instance) or in rooms too large for you to be heard easily at the back.

A microphone that is attached to a lectern or fixed to a stand severely reduces your scope for natural and fluid movement. If possible, try to get hold of a radio microphone, which transmits the signal through a small radio antenna rather than through a wire. Alternatively, you may want to use a lapel microphone, especially in panel or interview situations. This has the added advantage that you do not need to learn how to hold the microphone – you simply clip it to your lapel and forget all about it.

You should always check with the organizers of the event whether or not they expect that you will need to use a microphone. On the day, conduct your own experiment to check whether you can be heard at the far extremes of the venue. Remember, however, that your audience's clothes will absorb sound, and so even if you can be heard in the room when it is empty, people at the back may find it difficult to hear you when the room is full.

If you find that you cannot get away without using a microphone, it is essential to practise, not only at home, but with the microphone at the venue. You must learn to set your voice to the right volume, and you must find out how far away from the microphone you can move before your voice gets lost. Teach yourself to avoid feedback, that distressing high-pitched squeal some systems give out when you move the microphone in front of the loudspeaker, and find out how slowly you must speak to be understood through the echo of a public address system.

WARNING

Always, always beware of microphones that are switched on when you thought they were switched off. Microphones have a nasty habit of picking up unfortunate comments not intended for broadcasting.

Presenting visual aids

If you have incorporated any form of visual aid into your presentation, you will need to pay particular attention to your body language. Your first consideration should be not to allow the visual aid to come between you and the audience.

Too many speakers bend down to read overhead projector transparencies, or turn their backs on the audience in order to see which slide is on the screen. However great the temptation to do otherwise, always speak to the audience, and not to the equipment. You will help yourself if you make it a rule never to operate the visual aid (to write on the flip chart or to scribble on overhead projector transparencies) while you are speaking. If you are showing slides, use a mirror that clips to your lectern or stands on the table, and angle it so that you can check the screen behind you without turning round.

The second problem with presenting visual aids is that they seem to offer untold opportunities for nervous speakers to fiddle. If you have to do something like change a transparency or 'reveal' an exhibit, do so with as little extra movement as possible. Practise changing transparencies in one slick movement – off with the left hand and on with the right. Make sure it is in position, and then do not touch it again until you come to replace it with the next transparency. Make sure before you start speaking that your aids are in place and in order, and remember that if you need something to point with it is to hand.

Time for rehearsal

Skilful use of equipment such as microphones and visual aids can be learned through practise and familiarity. In the same way, all the techniques that combine to make a good delivery – effective use of notes, understanding and controlling the body and voice – can be assimilated through rehearsal, until they come to be second nature. Conscious use of these techniques, however, could make you seem ridiculously unnatural. Equally, preparation through rehearsal makes you familiar with the situation you are likely to find yourself in when you rise to speak, and will go some way towards reducing your nerves.

It is essential, therefore, especially if speaking in public is a new experience, that you devote some time to rehearsing. Depending on your schedule, you may have a little or a lot of time in which to rehearse. Rehearsals need not take a long time, just an hour or so every session, depending on the length of your speech. It is, however, important to leave, say, a week before you are due to give your speech in which to do this.

What follows does not constitute a rigid rehearsal programme that is guaranteed to produce a perfect performance on the day, but it does give some idea about how to rehearse your speech effectively. Remember that you are not trying to commit the whole of your speech to memory, but simply to integrate all the elements of good delivery so that they appear natural. This involves experimentation (trying out words and phrases, and combining them with different gestures or expression) and memory (remembering to use the combinations that you have discovered).

What to look for in rehearsal

There are several stages in a progressive rehearsal of a speech. You may begin with the full script of the speech in front of you, or simply notes, and you may intend either to 'read' from the script on the day, or to reduce it to note form. Here are some suggestions for what to look out for at each stage. Whatever stage you are at, it is always a good idea to stand up and try to deliver the speech to an imaginary audience, rather than whispering the words to yourself as you hunch over your desk. It is also a good idea to rehearse with your visual aids right from the start.

1. At the first stage, you are working either from notes or from an annotated script. Read through. Try out alternative phrases and descriptions, add pauses, and try to decide whether your speech hangs together as a logical and coherent train of thought. Note down any changes, and try the whole thing again. It may take you a number of read-throughs before you are happy with the content of your speech.

Ask yourself these questions:

- Is this speech about the topic I have chosen?
- Is there anything superfluous that I can cut out?
- Is this speech appropriate to the audience and the occasion (see pp.15–21)?
- Am I using the right visuals for the right reasons (see pp.59–66)?
- Is this speech likely to help me to achieve my objectives (see pp.10–14)?

Time your speech. Make sure that it is shorter than the time limit you have been given – you need to leave time for audience reaction. Make any cuts necessary to ensure that you do not run over time. If you run short, you can always fill in time by taking questions, but running over time is a sin that is not often forgiven.

When you are certain that the material and basic form of your speech is right, transfer it to cue cards, or whichever form of notes you have chosen. If you are already working from notes, it would be a good idea to rewrite them, to take account of the changes you have made. If you intend to work from the script, you may need to retype it.

2. From this point on, try not to add anything to your notes or script. (Remember that they take the form of key words only – you should now be working to extemporize from them successfully.) Run through the speech a couple of times more. If you have picked out a couple of sentences that you would like to learn by heart, do it now.

Keep experimenting with new words and phrases. Work hard to draw out each thought into a full picture of what you mean to say.

PRACTISING HUMOUR

The only thing that you cannot rehearse is humour. Jokes require an audience for you to gauge how they might go down. Try out the humorous elements of your speech on friends and colleagues.

PRACTICAL TECHNIQUES

Vary the pitch, pace and volume of your voice (it helps if you can rehearse in a quiet room away from distractions).

Are you happy with the memory aid that you have chosen to use? Are you only glancing at your notes or script to remind you of the next idea?

3. At this stage you might like to record your speech, so that you can analyse the aural element of your delivery. Don't play back straight away; leave it an hour or so, then you will come to it with a fresh mind, the better to analyse what you hear. Listen hard and ask yourself the following questions:

- Are you speaking slowly enough?
- Are you varying the pace slightly?
- Are you making good use of pauses?
- Do your sentences turn down at the ends?
- Are you giving the right kinds of expression to your words?
- Are there places where you are having difficulty expressing yourself?
- Do you use fillers: er, um, y'know, y'see?

Check the timing again – it is very easy to over-elaborate once you are at ease with your material.

Run through a couple more times, trying out remedies to the faults you have detected.

4. Next, draft in a friend who is able to take in the whole experience of your delivery – your appearance and message as well as your voice. Ask him or her to be as objective and as constructive as possible in their criticisms. As you deliver the speech again, imagine that your friend is in the middle of a mass of people. Practise looking around the room, only occasionally making eye contact with your friend.

Ask your friend what he or she believes your message to be. Get an opinion on jokes and anecdotes, and ask if you used any words that your friend did not understand. More than that, was there any line of thought that was rambling and confused?

Prime your friend to watch your movements – your body language and your gestures. Ask him or her to interrupt you every time you display a habitual movement or 'fillers' in your speech.

Some people use video recorders with which to record and analyse their physical appearance. The only disadvantage in this is that you are not able to get an objective opinion on the material you are using.

BE RUTHLESS

Don't hang on to material simply because it is a fond memory or a favourite anecdote. If you find that it doesn't work, throw it out.

---

5. You should be getting pretty close to the appointed hour by now – a little more polish, and you should be ready. At this stage, you may need to rehearse with technicians or other speakers. If this is the case, remember that this rehearsal should go just as the actual speech is planned to go. You might even wear the clothes you plan to wear on the day – who knows, you may discover that you have to walk up the steps to the podium crabwise because your skirt is too tight and the steps too high! Take the opportunity to get the feel of the venue, it will help enormously with nerves.

PRACTICAL TECHNIQUES

If you are thoroughly rehearsed, you should feel comfortable with your material. Your gestures and facial expression should flow naturally from your meaning. You should be able to control the length of pauses for effect, and you should be adept at glancing down at your notes to pick up the next train of thought. However, your speech should not have turned stale on you. It should be fresh and different every time you speak it. Keep it spontaneous and conversational.

Now the time is drawing close. You have researched and written your speech. You have directed it towards your audience, and you are clear in your objectives. You have rehearsed progressively over the past week or so, and your material is logically ordered to the best effect.

All you have to do now is to control your nerves and on the day make some last-minute checks, and deliver the speech to a real live audience.

KEY POINTS
Keep it:
✓ **conversational**
✓ **natural**
✓ **energetic**
✓ **enthusiastic**
✓ **spontaneous**

DEALING WITH NERVES

The first section in Practical Techniques dealt with the kinds of questions you may need to consider when faced with an invitation to speak in public. You may remember that fear of speaking in front of an audience was ruled out as a deciding factor. The reason for this was simple: fear need not become an obstacle to your success as a speaker. Indeed, nervousness can become a positive aid to your ability to put across your message, as long as you learn to take control of it.

Why persevere in the face of fear?

In moments of blind panic it may be difficult to remember why it ever occurred to you that you wanted to speak in public. Thousands of people stand up in front of some kind of audience every day – teachers, sales people, managers, priests, barristers, local group leaders, members of pressure groups, members of parliament – the list is endless. Each of these individuals has a different reason, and each gains some advantage by doing so. When they go out to fulfil their audience's needs, they are also fulfilling needs of their own: the need to make money; the need to protect their own physical or political freedom; the need to be accepted by their social group.

Learning the skills required to be a successful public speaker has many advantages:

- You become more effective in your workplace.
- You are better able to recall important facts and figures.
- You are better equipped to research information.

PRACTICAL TECHNIQUES

- You become more widely knowledgeable as a result of keeping your eye more closely on the media.
- You are better able to argue your point.
- You are better able to communicate with other people on many different levels.
- You can improve your interview or selling technique (although these are not covered in this book).
- You may find that other people consider you more interesting and seek out your company more often.
- You may have the opportunity to pass on your interest in a subject to other people.
- You may be able to persuade people to a good cause.
- You may find yourself making people laugh – one of the greatest gifts of all.

Whatever your reason, remember it when you are beset by nerves. If you have a good enough reason to speak in public, you will succeed in fulfilling your audience's needs and your own.

What are you frightened of?

The best way to describe how a person feels when they are frightened is to list a number of symptoms: sweating, blushing, racing pulse, clumsiness or shaking limbs, a blank mind. These symptoms tell you that your body has gone on red alert: this is the well-documented fight-or-flight response to danger. The key to fighting debilitating fear is to think beyond the symptoms to the cause.

When asked to list the reasons why they are frightened to speak in public, even in front of a small group of close colleagues or friends, people put forward a number of reasons:

- I am inexperienced.
- I do not know enough about the subject.
- I am afraid of the audience.

- My mind may go blank.
- The equipment may go wrong.
- I may make a complete fool of myself by saying or doing something stupid.

All these worries, and any others that may occur to you in the weeks leading up to your speech, are founded on one fear, the fear of the unknown.

As a novice speaker, making your debut, you may consider yourself in a particularly frightening situation. However, every speaker you have ever heard once made a maiden speech, and the debuts of some later very fine speakers were truly disastrous. The fear of the novice quickly disintegrates as soon as that maiden speech is over, so you may as well take the bull by the horns and do it now.

What else is there in the speaking situation that is unknown and therefore to be feared? You may feel that you do not know your subject well enough, or that you may lose your thread half way through, or, worse still that your mind will go blank the moment you stand up. However, it is in your hands to blow this fear completely out of the water by thorough preparation.

If you are not sure of your subject – take action to change it. You may be able to do this by narrowing the field so that you cover only those facts of which you are certain. Otherwise you may have the freedom to completely change the title and subject of your speech, and you should consider this a real option.

If you think you might lose your way, take time to rehearse well in advance, so that you can extemporize with ease. Extemporization is merely elaborating a theme. You do that every day, talking to the butcher about the price of lamb chops, or to your work colleagues about a newspaper article or last night's television. If you know your subject well enough, if you have planned your speech logically, and if you have made good

PRACTICAL TECHNIQUES

memory-jogging notes, you should have no fear of not finding your way back to the right path should you stray for a
moment.

Equally, there is no excuse for the fear that your equipment
might fail you. Familiarity with the equipment you intend to
use, and thorough checking of that available at the venue should
put your mind at rest.

Do you feel terror at the thought of the audience – all those
faces watching your every move, hanging on every syllable, just
waiting for you to put a foot wrong? You should be writing
horror fantasy, not contemplating speaking at your daughter's
wedding. Remember that each member of your audience has
decided that they would like to hear you speak. They are expecting to hear something that will fulfil at least one of their needs. If
you are truly sure of your subject matter, nobody should be able
to hold you up to ridicule. And very few people in the audience
are capable of doing any better than you if they were standing in
your shoes.

You think that you might stumble over your words, or get
your tongue twisted. Remove everything in your speech that
you might find difficult to get your tongue around (especially in
the opening sentences, when your anxiety will be at its height).
If you do stumble, don't apologise. Simply pause, take a deep
breath, remember what you were going to say, make eye contact,
and continue. Even the most experienced newsreaders stumble
over their words once in a while.

Picture the audience listening intently to your every word,
laughing uproariously at your merest quip and nodding sagely at
your deepest-held opinions. Fix an image in your mind of a
group of smiling, friendly people, who are truly pleased to listen
to your speech. Think positive!

Worst-case scenario

If you are still nervous of the unknown, try thinking of the worst thing that could possibly happen.

Think of the worst speech that you have ever heard, or remember the worst stage act you have ever seen. But **you** are prepared, you have something to say and you know how to say it. Your performance can only be better than those flops. Perhaps the worst thing that can happen is that you will bore your audience, or lose their attention. Surely if you lose their attention they will have forgotten all about you and your speech by the time they wake up next morning.

Perhaps for you, the worst case might be that you lose control in some way. However, bear in mind that you have already worked hard to make your speech a kind of conversation. Do you lose control when you have a normal everyday conversation? Then there is no reason why this conversation should be any different. In fact, there is even less chance that you will lose control over this particular conversation, because you know exactly what you are going to say well in advance.

Take every opportunity to be heard in public (only if you have something to say that is worth hearing, however). Say your piece at public meetings, call phone-in radio shows, have yourself nominated to the Church Roof Repairs Fundraising Committee. Prepare to speak impromptu at every occasion. Speaking on the spur of the moment is a good way to increase confidence because it has the added advantage that you are given very little time to think about refusing.

Practical ways of controlling fear

So you know now, if you did not already know, that fear is merely the product of feeling unprepared for the task ahead. However, fear is not a rational sentiment, it is a physical response, and try as you might, sometimes you simply cannot prevail.

An alternative method of tackling anxiety is through the body, rather than through the brain. People are more prone to anxiety in certain circumstances, and if you can avoid those circumstances, then it is possible to reduce stress significantly.

General health

Because fear is a physical reaction, people often find that when they are feeling below par, they become anxious about trivial things. Especially in the days leading up to your speech, rest well and eat properly. Take a couple of brisk walks, but beware of exercising more vigorously than usual.

The older a person becomes, the more their body relies on routine. When your routine is disrupted, your body experiences a certain amount of stress. Try not to change your habits. Do not stay up late every night working on your speech, when you normally go to bed at 10 pm.

Try to avoid too many stimulants: caffeine, cigarettes, etc. Your body is already stimulated with anxiety. Do not add to its load. Stay away from drugs of any sort, except where they are prescribed by a doctor. Do not take tranquillizers before you speak, they may have the effect of relaxing you, but they will probably relax you too much, and then you are seriously at risk of losing control. In the same way, try to avoid drinking too much alcohol on the day. You may find this particularly difficult if you are speaking at a social occasion such as a wedding or after dinner. A good rule is that one glass of wine is enough.

Learn a good breathing exercise, and practise it regularly. You will find that, apart from improving your ability to control your voice, the extra oxygen will steady your nerves. Watch your posture, an upright position, whether sitting or standing, will enable you to draw enough breath to control your nerves. Find a comfortable position and you will relieve tension in your muscles.

Positive use of fear

In seeking to reduce your anxiety, it is not necessary to eradicate it altogether. A taste of nerves keeps your brain alert, and it is important to stay on your mettle if you are to appear at your best.

The watchwords when it comes to combatting fear, then, are preparation and enthusiasm. Good preparation will reduce the risks of the worst-case scenario unfolding itself, and enthusiasm for your subject will ensure that you, if nobody else, has a good time.

Most of all, remember that you have very little to lose and a great deal to gain by speaking in public.

KEY POINTS
√ **think positive**
√ **do it now**
√ **be thoroughly prepared**
√ **stay fit and healthy**
√ **avoid drugs and stimulants**
√ **enjoy yourself**

PRACTICAL TECHNIQUES

ON THE DAY

All of the foregoing – from deciding to accept that first invitation, through studying your audience, to putting together and rehearsing your speech – has been leading inexorably towards one particular day, circled in red on your calendar. It is inevitable that as this day approaches, even relatively experienced speakers will become nervous. The following advice is aimed at reducing the possibility that something may go wrong, and at giving you every chance to control nerves and perform to the best of your ability.

Confirmation

In the week preceding the event, contact the organizers to confirm that all the details already supplied to you are correct, and that nothing has changed:

- Name and address of venue.
- Travel arrangements: parking space; street directions; who, if anyone, will be meeting you at the station?
- Contact name and telephone number should you be held up on the way.
- Time of the event – morning or evening?
- Dress requirements.
- Length of speech.
- Names of those to be mentioned in toasts.
- Special facilities if you are disabled.

Don't be fobbed off by harassed organizers who would simply like to tell you that nothing has changed since the last time you spoke. Make sure that the information is repeated over the phone, if not written down and faxed or mailed to you.

You must also confirm in writing the arrangements that have been agreed as regards a fee and payment of expenses. Find out who is going to pay you, and where you should send your receipts. Find out also when you can expect to be paid.

If you anticipate taking large pieces of equipment with you to the venue, and you expect that you will need someone to help you to carry them from your car to the platform, ask the organizers in advance to arrange for someone to do this.

At the same time as you confirm, put some thought into what you are going to wear – the night before will be too late to dry-clean a soiled dinner jacket or have your favourite pair of shoes repaired. By the same token, if you are planning to travel by car, make sure that it is not going to break down on the way. This might be a good time to take it to the garage for a service.

On the eve

Apart from the seconds before you rise to your feet to speak, the evening before can be the most stressful time as you anticipate the possible horrors of the following day.

Many people leave their final checks to the day of the speech. However, if action kills fear, it is a good idea to use the evening before to check your speech, equipment and clothes, and to get the best night's sleep you can. The best advice for the evening before the event is to stick as far as possible to routine. Don't go to the gym and pump iron for three hours if you normally only work out for one – you will end up exhausted and make yourself vulnerable to anxiety. For the same reason, don't make a start on long or arduous tasks in an effort to divert your attention elsewhere.

Many people try to allay their night-before fears by shutting themselves away and practising their speech over and over again. At this stage, such practise only increases stress and may end in your speech becoming stale. Practise your speech only once on the night before. This should not be a 'dress rehearsal'. Just work through your notes point by point, all the time trying to find new words and phrases that will freshen up your delivery. Resist the temptation to make any sweeping changes at this stage – your speech should have been firm in its structure and substance long before now. Check that all the leaves of your script or all the cards in your pack are present. When you have finished, put your speech out of your mind.

The eve of your speech is also a good time to check all your visual aids. Make sure that equipment is working, and that you have all the material – transparencies, slides, etc. – that you require. Check that you have the right number of handouts. Do all your felt-tip pens work? Now put all your visual material aside, or even lock them in the car ready for the morning. When you have done this, put your visual aids out of your mind.

Now take time to lay out your clothes for the occasion. Check the fine details, such as missing buttons and fraying shoelaces. When you have made any repairs and pressed any creases out, stop thinking about your clothes.

You have checked your clothes, your visuals and your speech, and everything is in place. You are sure that the details for the journey are correct, and you have worked out how you are going to organize your day in order to be on time. So why worry? Now is the time to relax.

Try simply to rest, avoiding strenuous activities. Slumping in front of the television may not seem strenuous, but poor posture in front of the box can create tension in the body, and a long stretch goggling will make your eyes tired. Equally, a night on the town may take your mind off the coming ordeal, but it will by no means encourage restful sleep and a focused mind in the morning. Perhaps a long bath and a book would be a good idea, or an hour or two beside the radio or listening to music. Do something that you enjoy.

Go to bed at your normal time and, unless you take them regularly, avoid sleeping pills. Try instead herbal tea or hot milk. A short walk before bedtime may also help to blow away the cobwebs and prepare you for a refreshing night's sleep. If you still cannot sleep for the butterflies in your stomach, try a breathing exercise to calm yourself.

Setting out

Make sure that you give yourself enough time to reach your destination. If your journey is a long one, rather than, say, a drive into town, add about half an hour to the timing. Aim to arrive at the venue at least an hour in advance – you will need this time to make your final preparations and perhaps meet members of the audience or the host organization.

> **Set your watch and make sure that it is keeping time properly – it is just as invaluable a piece of equipment as a slide projector or a flip chart.**

Before you leave, check that you have everything that you might need:

- your speech – cue cards, script or crib sheet
- your spectacles
- a notebook containing the contact number should you get lost or break down, and the details of the travel arrangements. You may also find this useful for noting down last-minute thoughts, phrases and ideas that occur to you while you are travelling

PRACTICAL TECHNIQUES

- a pen or pencil
- some tissues
- small change for telephone calls and parking charges

> If you are speaking in a new town, try to pick up a
> copy of the local newspaper on your way to the
> venue – you may find that it yields useful
> information, and it will endear you to your
> audience if you seem to know something about
> their town.

On arrival

As soon as you arrive, announce yourself to the organizers, get a
few minutes of their time, and check the following points:

- Have there been any last minute changes of running order –
what time are you expected to speak?
- Are the people to whom you will be referring still expected to
attend? You may have written in a funny anecdote relating to a
friend of the bride, and if he has just become seriously ill, it
may be considered bad taste to use it. Check again the names
of the people you must mention when proposing a toast.
- Are members of the press or other media expected to attend?

If you are expecting to be introduced, ask to speak to the person
who will be performing that function. Check that he or she has
got the facts right, and that they are using only relevant information – you do not want your audience to be asleep even before
you have stood up.

Checking out the venue

At the earliest possible opportunity, pay a visit to the room in which you will be speaking. Take a look at the way the room has been organized and find out where you will be speaking from. Check that you and your visuals can be seen from every seat in the room – do it yourself by sitting in all the most extreme positions (at the back and at the ends of rows). Take whatever action is necessary to make sure that everyone can see.

If you have been positioned in front of some distraction, such as a window, ask whether it is possible to be moved, or to close the curtains.

Make sure that you do not have to turn your back on sections of the audience in order to make eye contact with others. If you do, you may have to ask that the seating is moved. Changes of this nature may well not be possible, especially at dinners, where the guests are often seated in scattered clusters, but if you cannot do anything about the problem, at least you are aware of it, and know that you will have to work that little bit harder to make eye contact and draw the audience into a cohesive whole.

If you have not already had a dress rehearsal, talk to the technician, and if necessary, run through your script and slides or sound with him or her.

Check that the lighting and air conditions are suitable. If you are speaking into a darkened hall (perhaps if you are showing slides) make sure that the lectern has a light which illuminates your face. Also check the height of the lectern, and of the easel on which you plan to place your flip chart.

If the room feels too hot or too cold, ask to have the air conditioning modified. A cold and irritable audience is just as bad as one that is hot and sleepy.

Listen for audible distractions. Perhaps there is a bar or kitchen adjoining the room in which you will be speaking. If this is the case, you may have to ask that someone makes sure that catering staff stay quiet while you are speaking. If there is a telephone in the room, check that it has been unplugged, or that the relevant telephonist has instructions to bar calls to this number. If there is a noisy air-conditioning system, ask if it can be turned off (without causing undue discomfort) when you are speaking.

You may have time to rehearse the opening of your speech. Don't do this when there are too many other people around, especially members of the audience. If there is an opportunity to rehearse, ask someone to tell you whether you can be heard at the far end of the hall. Check that your microphone is working, and that it is correctly positioned.

If you are not to be seated in a special position before you speak (on the platform, for example), reserve yourself a seat as close as possible to the speaking position. Practise walking briskly from your seat to the speaking position.

Find out where the lavatory is – you will probably need to use it shortly before you speak. Make sure that there is drinking water available in an accessible position.

Of course, if you are only one of a number of speakers lined up for the day, it may not be possible to carry out some of these checks, or to position your visuals beforehand. However, do as many as you can, so that you have to do as little shuffling as possible when you stand up to speak.

If there are members of the press present, ask to be introduced to them, and offer to be interviewed after you have given your speech. In this way you will be able to clarify points in your argument, and to ensure that journalists do not make any mistakes when reporting your speech.

Being sociable

When you are satisfied that all the on-the-spot arrangements are complete, you may have time to socialize. You may be asked to join your hosts or gathering members of the audience for a drink, for example, or you may be expected to join the guests for dinner. This is a very useful time. If members of the audience see that you are mingling with them in an affable sort of way, you will reinforce the feeling that you are a friendly and sympathetic person who is interested in the event taking place and in the people in the audience. It will also take your mind off your speech and enable you to judge the mood of your audience. Make use of interval periods in the same way.

If you are offered a drink, take one – preferably wine rather than spirits – but only one. Eat sparingly, and try to enjoy yourself.

If you are in the hall when the audience are taking their seats, keep an eye on their distribution. A small audience that is scattered across a large auditorium is going to be difficult to handle, whereas a number of people in a tight group react more clearly to a speaker. For example, laughter is transmitted from one person to another more readily if they are in close proximity to one another. You will also have to work hard at making eye contact if the audience is fragmented. If necessary, ask one of the stewards to request that people move forward and close ranks.

Final countdown

A few minutes before you are due to speak, begin to prepare yourself. Now is the time to make that final trip to the lavatory, perhaps to splash your face with cold water. Alternatively, leave the building altogether and walk a few brisk steps across the car park, breathing deeply. This will freshen you up and clear your mind for the task ahead.

If you have to sit through other people's speeches, be alert and interested. You will probably be just as visible as the person currently speaking, and so you must do nothing to distract the audience's attention. You may also need to edit your speech, perhaps to cut a point that the previous speaker has already made, or to make sure that you refer back to that speaker if you disagree. Keep an eye on the time – if a previous speaker goes on too long, you may need to cut your speech.

Also, use this time to drink in the atmosphere, and judge the mood of the audience.

When you are being introduced, look at the introducer, and keep an open, alert face. Don't mime a reaction to what the introducer is saying. While the introduction is being made, breathe deeply and concentrate on the opening words of your speech. Become alert in readiness. When the introduction is over, get into position, make yourself comfortable, check that you have the audience's full attention, smile, take a breath and begin.

If you are using the same space as a previous speaker, make sure that you clear up after them – wipe the blackboard, remove litter such as coffee cups and waste paper. There should be nothing to remind the audience of the previous speech which may distract attention from what you are saying.

Dealing with hecklers

Some people come to meetings with the aim of disrupting the proceedings. Others may become boisterous with drink. Dealing successfully with such unwanted elements is an essential skill. It is your task to maintain the audience's (and your own) concentration, so that they do not get lost, and also to stay in control of the proceedings.

If you have the opportunity before you speak, observe the audience, and note anyone who is likely to disrupt your speech. Work hard to grab their attention in particular once you start speaking.

The first time you are heckled, it is best to ignore it, or to smile in response to audience laughter. Try to regain audience attention immediately, but make sure your next words are not lost in the disruption. Repeat the last thing you said to pick up the threads of your speech.

If you are interrupted a second time, be prepared with a put-down – witty rather than aggressive remarks are always the most successful. If you envisage a rough ride, you might have a few prepared and scribbled onto your notes just in case. You might be mildly insulting, or you might call upon the people close to the heckler to take control of him or her. In this way you isolate him or her, drawing the rest of the audience firmly onto your side. It is essential that you are quick with your remark, and that you say it loud enough to draw attention away from the disruptive element and back to the podium. Keep your sense of humour at all times. If you are seen to be rattled by a heckler, you will lose face.

Only if a heckler becomes abusive should you contemplate having him or her ejected. By this time, the master of ceremonies or chairman should have stepped in to ask for quiet and a little respect for you as a guest. If this is not enough to shame hecklers into submission, leave it to whoever is in charge to take action – a whispered word or a veiled plea should be enough to prompt this action. Never petulantly declare that you are not prepared to go on until the heckler is removed.

Heckling works by shaking the speaker's confidence, and hecklers rarely have anything of substance to say. Remember that you are the only person with enough courage to step onto the platform, and that you have something worthwhile to tell the audience.

PRACTICAL TECHNIQUES

Question time

You may find yourself in situations where it is possible for the audience to put questions to you. If this is the case, ask that the introducer announces this fact, and tells the audience when questions will be taken. Obviously, the best time to do this is when you have finished your speech to minimize disruptions. Also, if the audience is primed beforehand, they will be considering their questions as you speak.

The last thing many speakers want to do when they have finished their speech is to remain in the spotlight for a few minutes longer, open to the possibility of attack. However, question time can be useful for two reasons. First, it is an opportunity to clarify points that may have been misunderstood, and second, it gives you an insight into the audience's concerns, which you can use to improve your speech-making.

Many members of an audience feel uncomfortable when questions are called for. They feel intimidated at the prospect of standing up to make their opinions known. It is, after all, a form of impromptu speaking which requires as much practise and confidence as delivering a prepared speech. Be aware that your questioners are probably feeling uncomfortable, and use your body language to imply that you are receptive. You might shift your position so that things become less formal – perhaps you might sit on the edge of a desk.

If you are confronted with an embarrassed silence, you might try suggesting a question or two yourself. 'Many people have asked me whether I encountered any language difficulties when travelling in the Himalayas...', 'Perhaps you are wondering whether you could undertake this kind of journey...'. If you angle these questions properly, you will find that some members of the audience nod, in which case you can go on to give an answer. By doing this, you will break the ice and set the audience off on a train of thought that should bring an avalanche of questions.

One alternative way around the problem of the pregnant pause is to employ friends in the audience. If necessary prime them with pre-written questions to set the ball rolling.

You may have found out that there is an expert in the audience. (You may have found this out while socializing beforehand, or during a break between conference sessions.) If you are sure, and you know his or her name, call upon them to give their opinion, or invite them to add anything they think fit. This should ease audience tension and help to initiate a discussion of issues related to your speech.

When you take a question, listen carefully and try to repeat it, not only so that the whole audience can hear what has been said, but also to give you time to frame your answer. Make sure that you do get a question. If your questioner is rambling, you may have to formulate his or her question yourself – 'I think what you are asking is ...'. If you do this, ask for an affirmation of your formulation, and then go on to give an answer.

Be polite and attentive at all times. Some questioners may appear hostile, others may simply wish to impress the rest of the audience with their knowledge of the subject. Don't be drawn into arguments over the validity of your facts – simply restate your credentials and the source of your information. Never be hostile or aggressive. In the face of a personal attack, restate your credentials with as much confidence as you can, but remain polite. If you disagree with what someone is saying, say so, and move on.

If a rambler is going on too long, and their subject is not relevant, try politely to elicit a question by restating the subject of your speech. If this does not work, suggest that because his or her train of thought is going off the point, you would be pleased to discuss it later (but make sure that you do).

Spend as much time as you can with questioners who are being constructive, and as little time as possible answering those who want to demonstrate their own prowess or to argue with you. A questioner may ask you to provide information that you do not have, or to answer a question to which you do not know the answer. If you do not know the answer, or do not have the information, be honest, and say so. Don't be drawn into unknown territory – or you may well find yourself scalped by the Indians! Suggest that you will find out the answer and send the information on – make sure that you get a name and address, and that you note down the query.

Be on your guard against relaxing too much. If you do so, you may find yourself drawn into making slanderous remarks, or entering into one-to-one conversations. Think about your body language as much as you can – the audience still wants to hear and understand what is being said, even though the main event – your speech – is over.

The key to a good question time, therefore, is to remain in control, be polite and brisk, and never try to busk your way through.

The aftermath

When you finally sit down to that long-awaited round of applause, you may feel a sudden surge of relief – you have survived!

One word of warning: stay in control, especially while still in view of the audience. Avoid grabbing the nearest alcohol, you may become elated very quickly, and this is not desirable. The audience's scrutiny of you does not end when you sit down, and post-speech boisterousness may very well undo all the careful public relations you have hitherto built up.

Whether your speech was successful or not, don't engage in a post mortem with your nearest neighbour on the platform. The time to think about the experience is when you have left the venue. Stay alert for your audience's response, and take into account the concerns of your audience as they presented themselves during question time. Even if you were a smash hit, you may find that you can improve your speech even further. Beware of being too hard on yourself. Even if you did not achieve your primary objective, you may find that you have achieved one of your secondary objectives. Next time you will be less nervous and quite a lot more able to succeed.

Above all remember that there is one thing that you have managed to do – you have delivered a speech in front of a real live audience, and that is a success in its own right – an achievement not to be made light of.

ACTING AS COMPERE

Comperes are usually employed to link succeeding acts in a cabaret. They are often comedians, who rely on their material and their personality to keep the audience amused during interludes between the turns. The role of compere is the public-speaking role that is most closely related to performing in a show business sense.

A good compere has feet in both the performers' and the audience's camps. He introduces the performers before they come on, and comments on their performance when they have left the stage. A compere should not treat his role as an opportunity to take over the show, or to air a string of his own favourite jokes. Instead, he urges the audience to agree that everybody (himself included) is having a good time, and forms the cabaret into a coherent whole. If the audience is led to believe that the compère is on their side, and that he is enjoying the show, they will be more ready to follow his example.

As with all other speakers, the compere must be aware of what kind of people are in the audience and what the occasion is, and if he knows this, he should be able to make some apposite comments that draw the audience together.

The compere also keeps an eye on what is going on backstage, so that he can cover for hitches – problems with scenery changes, power cuts, late, missing or inebriated performers.

The skills required, therefore, are similar to those necessary for the master of ceremonies: the ability to think on one's feet and to ad-lib when the necessity arises. Additionally, the compere must be acutely aware of pacing, and the mood of the audience as it changes during the evening. If you are compering, aim to keep things light-hearted and to generate an intimate atmosphere without hogging the limelight.

See Also:
Acting as Master of Ceremonies
Impromptu Speaking

ACTING AS MASTER OF CEREMONIES

A master of ceremonies (or MC) is employed by the organizers of an event to ensure that its various stages are given some cohesion and that the event itself goes off smoothly and successfully. An MC would most likely be needed at formal social functions, such as a company dinner, or at conferences or courses.

An MC's duties

The MC does not organize an event, and neither does he (or, more often nowadays, she) take the place of the chairman or figurehead. The essence of the MC's job is liaison between all participants: the organizers, the chairman, catering and other support staff, and those attending – dinner guests, students, delegates.

Behind the scenes the MC is totally calm, dealing with crises and last-minute changes – a missing speaker, a faulty public address system, mutiny in the kitchens, straying delegates. She must ensure that everybody knows what is happening when the unforeseen occurs. Guest speakers will be looking to the MC to ensure that speaking conditions are as good as they can be, and to

---

If you are asked to act as MC at an event, make it a rule not to drink alcohol – you above all will need to keep your head when all around are losing theirs!

---

make them feel at home. She should meet and greet all speakers and ensure that their specific needs are attended to. (See p.108 on arrival in **On the Day**.)

The public role of the MC is to act as a link between the various stages of the event. At a formal dinner, she shepherds the guests into the dining area, and announces grace and the toasts. At a conference, she ensures that everybody is in the right place at the right time, and introduces the speakers. A good MC will make connections between one speaker and the next, in much the same way as a good speaker connects each part of his or her speech with a linking paragraph. She will ensure that the audience is not only receptive to what follows, but is also in the right mood. A lively audience may need to be quelled in order that they might be better able to take in some serious facts and figures. A subdued audience may need to be jollied up in preparation for some light-hearted entertainment. An audience whose members are likely to want to nap because they have just consumed a four-course lunch must be woken and kept awake.

The content of an MC's speeches is information. She must therefore be concise and to the point, and must be sure that she has all the facts right. She must not allow her own personality to upstage other speakers; while an MC should be genial, and sometimes amusing, she should not seek to mould the event to her own pattern.

In moments of crisis, the MC must be prepared to ad-lib, disguising the tension in the situation, and keeping the audience occupied until the event can get under way once more. The skill of impromptu speaking is therefore a necessary one to acquire if you are to fill this role.

Master of ceremonies is an unenviable role. Very few people notice when things are running smoothly, and when they go wrong, the MC is the focal point for panic and frustration. The

ROLES AND EVENTS

best MCs are often forgotten because they deliberately allow their own personalities to 'disappear' in the process of liaison and introduction, they always ensure that the limelight is vacated for the star turn – the speaker. However, the role does have its compensations: you will be able to practise the art of the impromptu speech, and you will have an opportunity to deal with audiences of many different types and moods, both invaluable experience for public speakers.

See Also:
Acting as Compere
After-dinner Speaking

AFTER-DINNER SPEAKING

The vast majority of formal dinner occasions are hosted by organizations such as companies, clubs, associations or charities. As on many other social occasions, almost all after-dinner speeches take the form of toasts and replies. In some instances, a guest speaker has also been invited, and in this case, an introduction will often be given. This section gives the form for speaking at a formal dinner, information on giving toasts on other occasions (at weddings, or at christenings, for example) appears under separate headings.

Organizing after-dinner speakers

It normally falls to the chairman to see that the list of toasts and speakers is drawn up, and that each speaker is introduced in the correct order. This does not necessarily mean that the chairman must be the person to perform these tasks, merely that he or she is responsible for seeing that they are done.

It may be undesirable for the chairman to be the person to introduce each speaker – if he or she has been jumping up to make introductions, the audience's interest may be lost when the time comes for the chairman's own speech. An alternative is to employ a master of ceremonies (see p.120) or a toastmaster to perform these functions.

Whoever is in control of the proceedings, it is vital that they have a good sense of timing and brevity. He or she must know how to speed the proceedings when they are flagging and how to wait for the right moment before moving on. He or she must also resist the temptation to say anything that is not directly to the point.

ROLES AND EVENTS

> **Before and during the toasts, make sure that all guests have full glasses – it is impossible to drink to someone's health if you have nothing to drink!**

Toasts – content

The main point about toasts is that they are intended as a celebration and a well-wishing. They should be kept short, up-beat and optimistic without any trace of sycophancy or excesses of self-congratulation. Try above all to be sincere in your praise (if you cannot, perhaps you are the wrong person for the job).

Those proposing toasts may wish to start with a humorous quotation or anecdote, but ensure that it is relevant to the occasion. Finishing a toast is simple; all you have to do is propose the toast using the appropriate formula, drink and sit down.

Replying to a toast is a little more difficult, in that it requires the speaker to respond to the proposer as well as deliver a short, prepared speech. Be ready to listen carefully to what the proposer is saying and to think on your feet. You may need to remove an anecdote from your speech because a previous speaker has already mentioned it, or you may need to make additions in order to comment on what has been said, which is always desirable. If you do need to make additions, it is best to insert them at the start of your speech, so that you can get them over and done with, before moving on to the speech you have prepared.

This system of toast and response makes it possible for comments to be passed to and fro, and, if the speakers are skilled, the result can be very entertaining. However, resist at all costs any temptation to enter into disagreements or disputes with other speakers. Ignore comments that you consider insulting or untrue and emphasize the points that you agree with, to maintain a contented, unified atmosphere.

> **Remember to bring an extra note card and a pen with you so that you have somewhere to make notes on foregoing speeches, especially if you are going to be replying to a proposer.**

When preparing to speak at a dinner, make sure that you do your homework. You will need to know the names of the relevant people (and how to pronounce them), and you will certainly need to find something to say that is relevant to the occasion. Avoid if you can giving lists of achievements – these only bore listeners. Instead, pick out some of the year's highlights, and present them from a personal point of view.

Make sure that you remember why you are on your feet. Don't get carried away by your own eloquence and then sit down, forgetting to propose the toast! Make sure also that the toast you propose is the toast you have been asked to propose. Adding and coupling names to it on the spur of the moment is incorrect and impolite, and you may well leave other speakers with a problem of repetition.

The number of toasts is decided by the organizers. However, if there are more than two or three, things may start to become wearing, so try to keep your speech short and sharp.

Saying grace
Most formal dinners still begin with a grace, said either by the chairman, a clergyman or another suitable member of the company. The chairman, master of ceremonies or toastmaster asks

the company to stand up while grace is said. After grace, the guests sit down and the meal can begin. If you are asked to say grace, choose one that fits the occasion. The majority of the company may be agnostics or atheists, so you may decide to use a grace that is less overtly 'religious' and more humorous. Some ancient university colleges have traditional graces, and you can find out what the appropriate form is from the organizers. If you are short on inspiration, you may find it at the local library – there are several collections of graces currently on the market.

Loyal and patriotic toasts

If there is to be a loyal toast – the toast to the monarch – it is always the first to be proposed. It is also the shortest of toasts, because it requires no preamble. The loyal toast is always proposed by the host or the chairman, who rises to his or her feet, raises a glass and declares: 'Ladies and gentlemen, the Queen'. The guests stand up, raise their glasses and respond, 'The Queen'.

A second loyal toast – to the royal family – is now becoming less common, but if it is included, it should come after the toast to the monarch. The exact form of the toast to the royal family changes from time to time, and it is the Queen who authorizes the form, which is then issued by Buckingham Palace. Again, this toast does not require any kind of speech.

On formal occasions, guests should not smoke until the loyal toast has been proposed, so organizers should make sure that it is done as soon as possible after the meal is over. After the loyal toast, the host should announce that guests now have permission to smoke.

At dinners that are related to the armed forces, a patriotic toast – either to the forces in general, or to one specific force – is usually proposed. As with the loyal toast, the proposer (usually the host) merely declares: 'Ladies and gentlemen, Her Majesty's Forces', or '... The Royal Navy', and so on. If you are called upon to respond to a patriotic toast on behalf of your force, you will be expected to make a brief speech of thanks. (Incidentally, the Royal Navy are not required to stand to drink a toast (even to the Queen), originally to avoid the problem of naval personnel cracking their heads on ship-board low ceilings.)

The rest of the toasts that are proposed at formal dinners should be prefaced with short speeches.

Toasting the host

At formal functions, the host is normally an organization. It usually falls to one of the guests, or to a junior member of the host organization, to propose the toast to the host.

It is obviously essential to know something about the host, and to keep in mind the reason for the dinner. If you are not a member of the host organization, you might be able to get hold of a copy of their annual report or some other publication, which will give you some idea of what they do. Alternatively, talk to the person who has organized the event. You may be from a related organization, in which case you might draw parallels or highlight differences between the two. Always try to mention the guests of honour if there are any. If not, the chairman or president of the host organization is counted as the most important person present, and you should mention him or her. Again, it is diplomatic to know something of the person who will be responding to the toast, and to mention him or her in the proposing speech.

Toasting the guests

A member of the host organization is expected to propose a toast to the guests. This involves introducing the guests of honour to the company and welcoming them and all the other guests to the event. Mention guests in order of precedence. Include those who have been invited because they hold particular positions (the Mayor, for instance), or as a recognition of certain services or successes. Introduce these guests individually, and be prepared to elaborate on their achievements in their official capacity (rather than their personalities or family lives). Other important guests may include titled people, prominent business people or government officials who have been invited as personal friends or acquaintances, and they should also be mentioned and welcomed. Remember to use the correct forms of address when mentioning important guests (see p.247).

Next, mention and welcome all the other guests. The company may be divided into groups (for instance, guests at a company dinner may be divided into departments: sales, marketing, accounts, etc.), so take advantage of this and find something good to say about each.

Toasting the chairman
This toast is to the head of the host organization – its chairman or president. It requires the most preparation, because it should be the most individual. The person who proposes the toast to the chairman must know about his or her career and character. Mention the personal qualities that have been of benefit to the organization, and the successful changes or projects that he or she has initiated or been involved with. Try to strike a balance between admiration and humour. Avoid being over-familiar or sycophantic. Avoid at all costs any possibility of embarrassing or offending the subject.

Civic toast
This toast is proposed when the civic head of a town or city is attending. It need only be a short toast, to which the civic head will respond. Reference should be made to the particular

(admirable) qualities of the civic leader in his or her official capacity. Remember that he or she is attending as a representative of the community, and not as an individual in his or her own right. The most important thing is to keep the toast politically neutral.

Toast to the ladies

This toast stands as a monument to the days when women attended formal dinners as escorts to their husbands. These days, it is very likely that such 'escorts' are both male and female. So if this toast is included, it is more appropriate to use it as an opportunity to thank the partners of company or club members, perhaps for their support over the past year.

Replies

Each of the above toasts (apart from the loyal toast) require replies, which should be made immediately following the relevant toast. The purpose is to thank the proposer and to make a short speech.

Reply on behalf of the host

This is normally made by a member of the host organization. Find out something about the person who proposed the toast. Introduce him or her, offer your thanks for their kind words, and perhaps elaborate on what they have said. You may like to tell the assembled company why this person was chosen to propose the toast. (Have they had particular successes? Are they the newest member of the company? Have they just been promoted? Do they have a strong contact with the host organization?) You may also like to tell the audience why you have been asked to respond. Wind up the reply by repeating your thanks on behalf of the host organization.

ROLES AND EVENTS

Reply on behalf of the guests

Once again, thank the proposer of the toast to the guests, and find something to say about him or her. The main task is to show that the guests are enjoying their evening, so be humorous if you can.

Chairman's reply

On many occasions, this is the most important speech of the evening. The chairman should use it to mention the successes of the past year and perhaps to give some idea of where the organization plans to be going in the year to come. Avoid giving lists, and make sure that you single out some members of the organization by name. It is also the chairman's job to thank the organizers of the dinner.

Reply on behalf of the 'ladies'

This speech could be used to make the partners of members of the organization feel at home. Try to mention common experiences. For example, if employees of a firm have worked late to complete a particular project, mention ruined suppers, orphaned children and suchlike, but keep it humorous and emphasize that the partners support their spouses in their work for the organization.

Introducing a guest speaker

Some organizations engage the services of a guest speaker – someone who may be connected with the organization, or who may have something of special interest to say. Perhaps your amateur operatic society has been asked to perform in your town's twin in Europe – the guest speaker may be the director of the twin town's own operatic society. Alternatively, the speaker may be a professional (some are more famous than others), engaged simply to amuse.

If you are asked to introduce the guest speaker, make sure that you find out who he or she is and why they have been invited. The speaker may have sent the organizers a potted biography around which you can build a short introduction. It is never true that a person 'needs no introduction'. Even if the speaker is the prime minister, you must make an effort to connect the event with the speaker and to give the audience a reason to listen. Most of all, the introducer's job is to welcome the speaker and set them off on the right foot.

> **All toasts require the speaker to mention at least one other person, either to propose that a toast be made, or to thank a proposer. Make sure that while you indicate with a movement who it is you are talking about, you do not address your speech entirely to him or her (one group or another), and ignore the rest of the audience. One hand movement or nod in the right direction is enough to do the job, then concentrate on putting your message across to the whole audience.**

The guest speaker

The primary objective of an after-dinner speaker's appearance is to be amusing (without turning the thing into a cabaret), and the major imperative is to be relevant to the occasion and topical. The brief is normally very wide-ranging, and so you will need to put in some work to define the subject for your speech. You might take it from the activities of the host organization, and include scandals and goings-on in the organization's industry or sector. You may mention recent stories in the media, or events taking place on a well-known soap opera. Find out as much as you can about the interests of your audience so that you can connect with their interests and concerns.

It is also useful to know something about the chairman, so that you can include a short anecdote (checked for veracity, of course).

The conditions under which many after-dinner speeches are given are sometimes difficult. The audience may by this time be fairly well-oiled (while you have stayed sensibly sober), and so you may encounter hecklers or other disturbances. You may also find that the audience is scattered about the room, seated at round tables in groups of eight, ten or twelve. This means that you will have to work hard to draw members' attention away from the events taking place in each group and to unite and focus their attention on you. It often happens that each table generates its own tiny society, with its own humourists and leaders. Try to pick out who these people are early on, and to control their behaviour with eye contact, and perhaps the occasional mention.

Vote of thanks

It is customary for a member of the host organization to thank a guest speaker on behalf of the organization. It is not necessary to summarize the whole of the foregoing speech, simply to show that you, as a representative of the audience found it interesting and amusing. This is one situation in which you will need to make some notes and be ready to improvise.

If the speech has been a great success, say so, but avoid being over-lavish with your praise. Even if the speech has been a total flop, do try hard to be sincere in your thanks. The vote of thanks usually ends with a call for applause.

KEY POINTS

✓ keep it short
✓ be ready to improvise
✓ be sincere
✓ avoid sycophancy
✓ be topical and relevant
✓ do your homework

See Also:
Acting as Compere
Acting as Master of Ceremonies
Chairing a Meeting

APPEALS AND FUND-RAISING SPEECHES

> **And money is like muck, not good**
> **except to be spread.**
> **Francis Bacon**

When it comes to giving to charity, most people would not agree with Francis Bacon. Especially in hard economic times, people are more interested in the good their money can do for them than the good it can do for others. This might seem a needlessly cynical view, but it is true to say that no person does anything, least of all part with hard-earned cash, unless it is in some way in their own interest to do so. It is not enough, therefore, to make an amusing and informative speech. Persuading people to give to charity is a skill in its own right.

Tap into people's needs

The chapter **Knowing Your Audience** (p.15) gave a list of the psychological needs that we all have. When people come to hear a speech, they are seeking to fulfil one of those needs. They are doing the same thing when they decide to give to charity. The needs that may be fulfilled by making a donation to charity are:

- Economic – the need to be financially better off or secure.
- Physical comfort – the need to be warm, fed and healthy.
- Psychological – the need to be free from worry and any form of psychological anxiety, including guilt.

● Acceptance – the need to feel that other people accept them as part of a social group.

As a fund-raiser, your most powerful weapon is to show in a subtle way that by making a donation, one of these needs will be fulfilled. You will find this easy or more difficult, depending on what your charity is. If it is an industry benevolent society, you will have an easier ride proving to members of that industry that one day they may need to call upon its services. Here are some examples:

● An industry benevolent society – economic needs; or a health-related charity – physical comfort needs. The society performs an increasingly important role in helping retired pattern-makers who are unfortunate enough to fall on hard times. We all hope that we may never have to do the same, but in these unpredictable economic times, who knows what may happen?

● Building a children's hospital in Cambodia – psychological needs. Many of us here tonight have children of our own. We hold them to be the most precious things in our lives, and we find ourselves worried to distraction when they fall sick. In this country, we are privileged to be able to afford health care, virtually on demand. In Cambodia, things are very different . . .

● A local charity – acceptance need. This charity is blessed with a number of tireless volunteers who are able to devote much of their spare time to it. Many of you, I know, are not able to do this – we have families to look after, and demanding jobs. But we can all make a contribution in money, if not in time.

Consider how you can tap in to people's own needs and fears, and (without being too obvious about it) use them to the charity's advantage.

Bring the point back home

Try to relate the work of the charity to the daily lives of people in the audience. Try to make it real to them. How would members of the audience feel if this happened to them or their child/dog/husband (what is the statistical likelihood of this occurring)? Have members of the audience come into contact with people in this situation – have they seen down-and-outs on the street, met people suffering from AIDS or cancer, noticed how many stray dogs there are in the neighbourhood? How would people's lives be different if they lived under a regime that did not countenance freedom of speech?

The work of the charity

It is obviously important to tell the audience what the charity actually does, and why it is worthwhile. Make sure that you establish the external need that the charity seeks to fulfil (in the same way that you would establish a need for your product in a buyer's mind if you were a professional salesperson). Show that there is a need: many children in Cambodia are victims of the continuing guerrilla war, but some provinces have few hospitals; hundreds of dogs are roaming the street causing a nuisance and in some cases a danger; those suffering from AIDS need special care and attention.

When you have established the need, show how the charity aims to meet that need. The charity's work is the 'product' that the supporter is buying on behalf of the beneficiaries.

You might also like to tell the audience what your role in the charity is, and how long you have supported it. You might also find that there is a grass-roots worker in the audience, and if you can, relate his or her experiences to the others present. Use this evidence of personal involvement to make the work of the charity more immediate.

Buying-power

If you have the information, tell the audience what each pound of their donation will buy. Many major charities do this – using newspaper advertisements to suggest that £40 will support a child in Somalia for two months, for example. Even if most members of the audience can only afford £20, they know what this money will do, and can congratulate themselves on helping to bring about a concrete result. Talk to the charity's officers, and find out if they can give you such ammunition.

More for less

Many people are very happy to think that they can get (or give) more for less – a version of the economic need. If donations to the charity enjoy some sort of tax shelter, say so (and make sure that the necessary forms are circulated). If the appeal is backed by a benefactor who has agreed to match donations pound-for-pound, say that too.

Picking the right moment

In order to spirit money out of people's pockets and into the collecting tin, you need to pick a moment when they are in the right frame of mind to make your appeal. Wait until they have enjoyed the hospitality on offer. A couple of drinks can wear down a person's resolve, and having accepted your hospitality, most people will also feel bound to make a donation out of politeness or gratitude.

Start the ball rolling

Rather like taking questions after a lecture, it is up to you to start the donations ball rolling. You might do this by announcing (or having the organizers announce) that you are yourself making a donation. (Whether you announce this or not, you really must make a donation, to show your sincerity.) Alternatively, find out if anyone in the audience has promised to make a donation, and announce that, with your thanks on behalf of the charity. Some fund-raisers go so far as to canvas donations in advance or to approach people at the event to persuade them to give, and then thank them from the platform. Be careful when mentioning the size of donations. This kind of announcement will set the level each person is prepared to pay to keep face, so make sure it is high enough!

These days, there is much emphasis on charities using the money they raise efficiently. Many supporters feel that their money is wasted if it is used to pay large numbers of administrators (or people like you to make speeches, for that matter). If you can, find out what percentage of money raised goes directly to the work. How much does it cost to administrate the charity, and how much to build the hospital/renovate the church hall? If the statistics show that the charity is doing its best to be efficient, use them. You might also like to have someone announce the fact that you are donating your speaking fee to the charity!

Don't be shy

The people who have attended your fund-raising event have been told that they can expect to be asked for money. Further, by supporting your charity, they are not doing good for the sake of their immortal souls. They are here because they want to fulfil one or more of their own psychological needs. Therefore, don't be reticent about asking for money. Be as brazen as you like, and don't make excuses for yourself. However, do be polite, and make people feel that you are truly (but not grovellingly) grateful for their generosity.

Delivery

Make use of eye contact to show people that you are speaking to each individual – you have identified every one of them, and no-one is going to be allowed to slink away without paying up!

Even if you read your speeches in other contexts, this is one speech that you must deliver without a script. You must bring to it your heart-felt emotion, and reading from a script is the surest way to fail. By all means use notes, but concentrate on your delivery. Convey enthusiasm, warmth and sincerity, aim to persuade and inspire.

KEY POINTS

✓ appeal to the audience's own needs
✓ make the work of the charity seem real and immediate rather than far away
✓ choose your moment
✓ don't be bashful
✓ be sincere, speak with enthusiasm

BIRTHDAYS AND OTHER FAMILY CELEBRATIONS

As on most family occasions, birthday speeches often take the form of toasts, proposed by a friend or, in the case of a young person, a parent. You may find yourself proposing this toast at an 18th or 21st birthday in particular.

Suggested format

Begin by announcing the occasion and introducing the guest of honour. Depending on your relationship to the celebrant, you may then go on to a theme of friendship or parenthood. Another theme might be coming of age as a crossroads or departure point in the journey of life, or any other age being one of its great landmarks. You might be able to find an anecdote that is humorous without embarrassing the celebrant. Praise his or her good qualities, without being overly flattering or untruthful.

End by conveying birthday greetings on behalf of the company and wishing the celebrant success and long life in the future. If appropriate, you might also wish to thank the organizers of the event.

A reply by the celebrant might include affection for parents, family and friends, or musings on how it feels to be growing steadily older. Thank all present for their kind wishes.

KEY POINTS

√ **choose an appropriate theme**
√ **give praise where praise is due**

BIRTHDAYS AND OTHER FAMILY CELEBRATIONS

This format can be used for most birthday occasions. With a little ingenuity, it can also be adapted for other similar family occasions, such as Bar Mitzvah, Confirmation and First Communion celebrations.

See Also:
Christenings

BURNS NIGHT

The anniversary of the birthday of Robert Burns on 25th January is celebrated by Scots as a patriotic festival, and there is much scope for public speaking during the evening revelries: the customary addressing of the haggis, the two graces and the toasts.

The first 'speech' to be delivered is the address to the haggis, using Robert Burns' own words:

Address to a Haggis

Fair fa' your honest, sonsie face,
Great Chieftain o' the Puddin-race!
Aboon them a' ye tak your place,
    Painch, tripe, or thairm:
Weel are ye wordy of a grace
    As lang's my arm.

The groaning trencher there ye fill,
Your hurdies like a distant hill,
Your pin wad help to mend a mill
    In time o' need,
While thro' your pores the dews distil
    Like amber bead.

His knife see Rustic-labour dight,
An' cut you up wi' ready slight,
Trenching your gushing entrails bright
    Like onie ditch;
And then, O what a glorious sight,
    Warm-reeking, rich!

Then horn for horn they stretch an' strive,
Deil tak the hindmost, on they drive,
Till a' their weel-swall'd kytes belyve
    Are bent like drums;
Then auld Guidman, maist like to rive,
    Bethankit hums.

Is there that owre his French ragout,
Or olio that wad staw a sow,
Or fricasse wad mak her spew
    Wi' perfect sconner,
Looks down wi' sneering, scornfu' view
    On sic a dinner?

Poor devil! see him owre his trash,
As feckless as a wither'd rash,
His spindle shank a guid whip-lash,
    His nieve a nit;
Thro' bluidy flood or field to dash,
    O how unfit!

But mark the Rustic, haggis-fed,
The trembling earth resounds his tread,
Clap in his walie nieve a blade,
    He'll mak it whissle;
An' legs, an' arms, an' heads will sned,
    Like taps o' thrissle.

Ye Pow'rs wha mak mankind your care,
And dish them out their bill o' fare,
Auld Scotland wants nae skinking ware
    That jaups in luggies;
But if ye wish her gratefu' pray'r,
    Gie her a Haggis!

ROLES AND EVENTS

Obviously, only a Scot would be able to declaim such a poem with the appropriate accent and understanding, and it is unlikely that a Sassenach would be asked to do so. If you are invited to address the haggis, it is only fitting that you should learn the poem by heart. Try to recite it with as much expression as you can, to enable those who do not know or may not understand the poem to do so.

Before the meal begins, the customary grace is said:

Some hae meat that canna eat,
And some wad eat that want it,
But we hae meat and we can eat,
Sae let the Lord be thankit!

When the guests have finally demolished the haggis and all other offerings, a second grace is said, heralding the round of toasts and other speeches to follow:

O Lord, since we have feasted thus,
Whilk we sae little merit
Let Meg noo tak' awa the flesh
And Jock bring in the spirit.

KEY POINTS

✓ **learn the address to the haggis or the graces by heart**

Toasts are convivial and celebratory, usually including a patriotic toast, a toast to Robert Burns and a toast to the 'lassies', and often a reply to the toast to the lassies. If you are asked to take part, find out from your hosts which toast you are expected to propose. One rule to be borne in mind by all Sassenachs – only a Scotsman is permitted to criticize Robert Burns!

Guests may then go on to recite some of Burns's poetry, and the evening usually closes with a round of 'Auld Lang Syne'.

See Also:
After-Dinner Speaking

BUSINESS MEETINGS – FORMAL AND INFORMAL

> The length of a meeting rises with the
> square of the number of people present.
>> **Eileen Shanahan**

The vast majority of meetings take place in a business context. They are part of the internal and external communication process that is so important to any company. A person's performance at meetings of this type can be extremely important. A good performance ensures increased effectiveness in the workplace, and can greatly enhance overall career prospects.

Business meetings are either formal (for example, between a company and its client, or internal 'prepared' meetings) or informal (mostly between members of a single department at a moment's notice). The only real difference between formal and informal meetings is one of context – the skills required are the same. To perform well, you will need to be prepared, capable of persuading and able to speak coherently at a moment's notice. If you have time to prepare, work on your contribution in the same way as you would prepare a speech for any other occasion (see Practical Techniques section).

Preparation for business meetings

Most formal business meetings are heralded well in advance. You should be told the purpose of the meeting and who is going to be present, and why. You may receive an agenda giving all the information you need to get started on your preparation, but if not (and this may well be the case with informal meetings), ask the person who has called the meeting. Some of the questions you might need to ask are:

- When and where is the meeting to be held?
- What is the purpose of the meeting?
- Who will be present, and what is their status?
- Have the other participants been briefed with necessary information?
- Why are you being asked to attend?
- How long is the meeting expected to go on for?

A meeting could have one of a number of purposes: problem-solving, decision-making, selling (ideas as well as products) or transmitting information. Work out which you will be expected to do and plan your contribution accordingly.

Knowing who the other participants are will enable you to build up a picture of their needs and interests, which you will have to take into account. This is most likely to be a mixed group, at least in terms of the corporate hierarchy. You may be confronted with a combination of colleagues, superiors and subordinates, and each has his or her own concerns. Understanding what these different concerns are will enable you to speak more effectively and, if necessary, be more persuasive. Spend some time talking to the other participants if you can before the meeting, to confirm or modify your assumptions.

Do not aim your speech at one group only. It may be tempting to level your arguments at your superiors, on the assumption that they are the people with power to improve your career prospects. However, this will not only irritate your peer colleagues and subordinates, it is also likely to be detrimental to your cause.

ROLES AND EVENTS

In order to have proposals of any sort accepted, you will need to have them agreed by all the people they affect. Therefore, consider all members of your audience as equals.

It is important that you know how much the other participants know about the subject in hand. If they know very little, you may have to spend time presenting information before you can move on to a discussion of the issues. If they have been fully briefed, you will waste time going over old ground. If it seems that there is information that participants should have in advance, suggest to the meeting organizer that it is circulated.

When you know who the other participants are, and you have found out their concerns and the information they already have, you should be able to start making assumptions about their attitude towards the subject in hand:

- Will there be a consensus of opinion on the subject?
- Who will be against and why?
- Who can you count on as allies to agree with you and support you?

Finding out why you have been asked to attend is vital. You may be expected to speak on behalf of your department, or to advise because you have a specific expertise. You may be expected to report on the progress of your project, or to explain problems, or to make recommendations.

If you are being asked to represent a group, make sure that you are prepared to do just that. Ask around – canvas opinion – and incorporate other people's ideas into your speech. You might even call an informal meeting of members of your department so that you can discuss their concerns.

Remember to formulate a concise statement of your own objectives with the other participants in mind, and when you have finished preparing your contribution, check that you have addressed as many of the concerns of others as you can. (See **Setting Objectives** p.10)

Structure your speech just as you would any other. Make use of appeals, links and summaries to reinforce the structure. Remember to state your credentials. Even if you are meeting with close colleagues, it is as well to remind them why you are the right person to be speaking on this subject. (See **Planning and Writing** p.32)

The art of persuasion

It may well be that the objective of your speech is to persuade – to 'sell' an idea or a product to other participants. Indeed, even if you are not a sales person by profession, you will probably find that you spend most of your working life persuading people to 'buy' things (ideas if not products). While this book is too short to set down all the techniques learned by salespeople, there is space for a few hints on persuasion.

Some notes on persuasion:

- Understand the other party's standpoint: gain their sympathy by showing that you understand.
- Establish a need: you cannot reach a solution if the other party does not agree there is a problem.
- Give suggestions and explain their advantages: relate your solution/idea to the needs of the other party, interpret exactly how it will change their life/working conditions/effectiveness.
- Gloss over areas of minor disagreement: do not let them get in the way of the major issue; broad agreement is better than no agreement.
- Emphasize areas of agreement.
- Encourage a conclusion: define it and allow the other party to agree without losing face.

ROLES AND EVENTS

- Avoid coercion and the 'hard sell'.
- Show that you are committed and enthusiastic about your idea/product/solution.

In discussion

An activity common to almost all meetings is discussion, during which participants air their views and standpoints and thrash out the pros and cons of new ideas. Discussion is vital to the communication process, but unfocused discussion is a waste of time and money.

A discussion is rather like a speech, except that it is made by not one speaker, but several. While a normal speech is structured to lay before the audience several defined stages in order, a discussion will range from one sub-topic to another. It is therefore the duty of each participant to keep the main object of the discussion in sight at all times, so that, like an orchestra, they all end on the same note.

Efficient discussion relies on the participants being well-informed and able to put their points coherently and concisely. Your performance in discussion is just as important as your ability to make a prepared presentation.

Points to remember for discussions:

- Be prepared: read the agenda and other information. Make notes on points you would like to raise. If you think that you will be called upon to present extra evidence, take it with you. You might also consider taking handouts for distribution at the meeting – but talk to the organizer first, and don't go over the top. In preparation, avoid becoming fixed in your views, consider what alternative arguments might be.

• Listen attentively to the other speakers, whether they are making a presentation or passing comment. Try to identify their viewpoint. If you can, test your assumption by asking questions: 'Are you suggesting that we buy a new photocopier?' 'Are you saying that we need to look again at the pay structure?' Make notes – you may not get a chance to speak at the very moment a thought comes into your head.

• Your body language should convey that you are alert and open to new ideas (sit forward on your seat and put your hands on the table – don't fidget).

• Never whisper while another person is speaking, and don't interrupt.

• Show that you value other people's ideas and that you respect their point of view. Never jump in as soon as a person has finished speaking. Leave a pause for thought to show that you are considering what they have said.

• If a person has already made the point you wanted to make, say that you agree with him or her, and perhaps add your own reasons.

• Use a similar formula to disagree with what someone has said.

• If you are introducing a new line of reasoning or a new idea, make sure that you relate it to the subject under discussion, in the same way as you would link two stages in a speech: 'We are here to discuss ways in which we might ensure maintaining the company's position in the industry. One idea that has been put forward is to upgrade our software. However, some members of my department have suggested that it might be a good idea to narrow the range of services we offer, and aim for excellence.'

● In general, it is the chair's role to direct the discussion and to make regular summaries to keep the meeting moving forward (see **Chairing a Meeting** p.160). If this does not happen, it might fall to you to do this. The best way to do this is to follow the suggestions given above when making your contribution. Avoid usurping the chair person's position, or taking control when this is not appropriate.

● Stay in good humour, even when your own pet ideas are being blown out of the water.

KEY POINTS
√ **be prepared**
√ **research the 'audience', and in discussion, keep other people's views in mind**
√ **learn to be persuasive, but avoid the hard sell**
√ **be courteous in discussion – show that you value other people's contributions**
√ **emphasize areas of agreement**
√ **remember the purpose of the meeting**
√ **never lose your temper**

Meetings cost money. Each participant is being paid to attend, and they are all putting aside their own work to do so. A member of staff who is good in meetings – who speaks to the point and does his or her bit to ensure that the meeting is efficient and productive – is invaluable to any company. Equally, business meetings can provide a good training ground – both for making prepared and impromptu speeches – for those who wish to use their skills elsewhere.

See Also:
Business Presentations
Impromptu Speaking
Panel Discussions
Seminars and Workshops

BUSINESS PRESENTATIONS

Formal presentations in a business context are for many people the cause of a great deal of anxiety. But success in business often comes down to a person's ability to give an informative and persuasive presentation. This should not be a matter for prayer – prepare to persuade your audience that it is in their best interest to accept your proposal, and you will be less likely to spoil your business.

Guidelines for a presentation

Business presentations are a matter of selling, regardless of whether your proposal has as its subject a product or an idea or plan. The audience may be members of your company's board of directors, or directors of a client firm. You may even be making a presentation to members of your industry as a whole. Whoever the audience is, it can be very daunting to be faced with a row of faces, each belonging to a person who could make or break your business or career.

Your aim is to get the audience to agree with you that your proposal is the right one for them, and to do this, it is important to enable them to agree with every stage of your argument. The most successful salespeople have the knack of making their audiences feel that they will be the ones taking the credit for instituting successful change.

Here are some guidelines:

• Be organized
Check out the venue beforehand, and make sure all your equipment, notes and props are in position. Make sure that the people

you are talking to are circulated with any background information in advance of the meeting.

● Be professional
Dress to impress, be polite and alert. Be formal, even if your audience is not. Do not smoke. Do not waste your audience's time.
Show you mean business.

● Defer to the chairperson
The chair of the meeting should introduce you to all those present (you should know in advance who is going to be present, and perhaps you should jot down the seating positions of everyone there so that you can address people by name). Allow the chairperson to run the meeting, and to handle other participants.

● Do not be overawed
While it is true that you are meeting the enemy on its own territory, and therefore suffer a minor disadvantage at the outset, do not become overawed. Stand up to give your presentation to make yourself the focus of attention.

● Give your credentials
Tell the audience why they should listen to you, and why they should believe in the accuracy of your information and the efficacy of your proposal.

● Make them say yes
If you are to get agreement to your proposal, it is useful to put the audience in a positive frame of mind. A time-honoured technique is to ask questions that make them say yes. Before you begin, tell them how long you expect to be speaking for, and

what the subject of your presentation is. Never frame your question for a no answer.

● Establish a need

You will never get anywhere in trying to sell your idea or product unless your buyers believe that they have a need for it. Establish the need by explaining the situation as it now stands (with evidence). Show that there is a problem that needs to be solved and get agreement that this is indeed a problem that should be addressed (make them say yes). Be prepared to go on to show how your idea can solve that problem.

● Speak to their needs and interests

Research the audience beforehand and work out what their needs and interests are: the need for profit; the need for increased market share; the need for efficiency; the need to protect their workers' jobs; the need to improve product quality. Just as there is no place for prayer in business, so there is no place for sentimental appeals. Cynical though this may seem, self-interest is a stronger motivation to action than charity. When establishing a need do so in your audience's terms. Make sure your arguments prove that the proposal will serve some if not all of your audience's needs.

● Consider alternatives

It is important to show that you have considered alternative solutions, and to tell the audience why you think yours is the best.

● Be accurate

Do your homework and check your figures. Be accurate, and make sure that you have made no mistakes in your calculations. In business, money is obviously one of the deciding factors in any transaction, so make sure you put a genuine price tag on your proposal.

● Pre-empt objections

Work out what the possible objections to your proposal might be: is the plan too costly? too time-consuming? too risky? Argue against them: 'You are probably thinking that this proposal is not worth the price, but I would like to show you some projections that prove that investment now means a disproportionate increase in profits in the long run . . .'

● Give evidence

Every single assertion that you make must be backed up with hard facts in evidence.

● Ask for action

In your introduction and again when you are summing up, tell the audience exactly what action you are asking them to take, and, if appropriate, on what timescale.

● Be respectful

Never put a member of your audience down. If someone interrupts your presentation with a question, do not snap back that you will take questions later. Tell him or her that you would like to lay out all the arguments before attending to queries. Ask him or her for permission to save queries until that time. Get a yes response. That person may have lost face, but at least he or she has been given an opportunity to show that they can be reasonable.

● Be honest

Don't allow anyone to doubt your motives for putting forward your proposal. No-one believes that a salesperson is proposing to sell customers something for their own good, without gaining something himself. Tell the audience why it is in your interest that your proposal is adopted (your department might benefit, it may make your life easier) in the same terms as you appeal to the audience's own self-interest.

● Be enthusiastic
Enthusiasm is catching. If you do not appear interested and committed to your proposal, why should anyone else believe that it is a good idea?

When you walk into the board room, it is likely that your heart will be in your mouth – it is the same for most people. Not only must you get through your presentation unscathed, but you must also get agreement to your proposal. The worst thing that can happen is that you are turned down. You will not be pelted with rotting cabbage or summarily dismissed from your post. Think positive, you can always try again, and next time you will arm yourself better against the objections that have been raised this time. You have nothing to lose by trying, and if you prepare

---

KEY POINTS

√ **prepare to be a sales person**
√ **prepare to present strong arguments**
√ **prepare to meet the needs of the audience**
√ **prepare to give evidence**
√ **prepare to pre-empt objections**
√ **prepare to be enthusiastic**
√ **prepare to get agreement**
√ **prepare thoroughly**

thoroughly, make a strong argument and appeal to the needs and the interests of your audience, there is no reason why you should not succeed.

See Also:
Business Meetings

Practical Techniques –
   Knowing your Audience
   Improving your Style
   Visual Aids
   On the Day

CHAIRING A MEETING

**Whether you call it chairman, chairwoman or just
chair, this role is a form of public speaking that
requires special qualities in the person who
chooses to accept it. Most important of all is the
ability to be able to listen when you really want to
speak.**

**Formal meetings, for example, of a company,
association or club, require the services of a
chairman, sometimes by law. Informal, for
instance, inter-departmental, meetings are not
bound to appoint a chairman, but they invariably
benefit from someone who is capable of directing
the thoughts and words of those present.**

**Chairmen must be good listeners. They must
also be fair, unerringly polite and good
timekeepers.**

Impartiality

Whatever type of meeting, it is essential that the chairman
remains impartial, and devotes his or her energy to guiding the
meeting, controlling speakers and ensuring an outcome. The
chairman should never comment on the substance of speeches
being put to the meeting, either for or against. Impartiality also
means not favouring one side over another by giving certain
speakers more time to be heard, or adjourning the meeting at a
particular moment for these reasons.

Make sure that both sides get a good hearing. You will soon be
able to pick out the strong personalities among those attending,
and to control them, while at the same time giving those who are
not so confident their say. You may wish to invoke the rule that a

person cannot speak twice on any given subject or motion. If you find this useful, state this rule at the start of the meeting.

The only time it is legitimate for a chairman to show which side he or she is on is when a casting vote is required. If you cannot be impartial – perhaps you have a special interest in the matter in hand – you should consider delegating the chair to someone else or not accept it in the first place.

Engendering respect

A chairman needs to be able to control those attending the meeting, and to enforce the rules when necessary. You cannot do this by brute force, so you must be able to do it by making the 'audience' respect you. Stay calm at all times, even when the debate is becoming heated. Try not to be heavy-handed or bullying when enforcing the rules. Be polite but firm.

Equally, do not let personalities get in the way. Treat everybody the same, whether they are your favoured drinking companion or the person who always rubs you up the wrong way. If someone becomes abusive rely on the point of order system to calm them down. In extreme circumstances, you may have to adjourn the meeting for ten minutes to allow frayed tempers to cool.

If you quietly enforce the rules, and make sure that your decisions and actions are always fair, you will be paid the respect the chair deserves.

Doing business

The aim of all meetings is to get through as much business as possible. We have all attended badly chaired meetings at which nothing was achieved but the interminable airing of oft-heard opinions. Perhaps a speaker has droned on for half an hour, or has digressed from the point. You must be able to bring such a person back into line quickly without seeming to be biased. One way of doing this is to set a time limit on each speech at the start of the meeting. In this way you can urge adherence to the general rule without seeming to single certain people out.

Always aim to move on as quickly as you can without cutting any corners. You will help yourself in this if you organize the meeting properly, ensuring that all the necessary information is to hand and that everybody who needs to be is present. If you are anticipating to take a vote any other way than by the show of hands, ensure that you have enough stewards to do the counting quickly.

Stand to deliver

If you are handling a large meeting, with those attending seated in rows in the body of a hall, rather than round a table, it is a good idea to ask all those who want to speak to indicate to the chair that they want to do so by raising their hand, and to stand and address the chair when they are putting their point. This gives the chairman three advantages. First, speakers from the floor can be heard better when they are standing than when they are sitting. Second, a person who is standing when everybody else is sitting is isolated from the group. He or she is less likely to be disruptive, abusive or longwinded without the camaraderie of the crowd (most people are so nervous about being exposed in this way that they cannot wait to sit down again). Third, when you can see who is doing the talking, you are better able to identify them and to ensure that they do not get more than their fair share of air time. Asking people to address their remarks to the chair also means that you have a polite means of stopping people getting into personal disputes among themselves.

Formal meetings

Formal meetings – AGMs, for example – are governed by law and by the bye-laws of the company, association or society that is meeting. It is essential that the person chairing these meetings understands such procedures and rules, so that the business of the meeting is transacted according to law. Irregularities in the proceedings may mean that decisions can be overturned at a later date.

It is very rare that anyone who is new to these kinds of formal meetings will be asked to chair one. Therefore, the complexities of motions and amendments, proposers and seconders, adjournments, closures and voting will not be explained here. However, the person to turn to if you are unsure of the form is the secretary (either the company secretary, or the honorary secretary), who will be able to tell you the form, and inform you as to the minutiae of the body's bye-laws. It is comforting to know that this person, often someone who has officiated at such meetings for many years, will be at your side on the platform when the time comes.

Formal meetings – the chairman's duties

The first responsibility of the chairman is to ensure that the proper notice of a meeting is given, according to the body's regulations. Such notices are sent by the secretary to all the members, and may also include the agenda for the meeting.

At the meeting itself, the chairman must ascertain whether there are enough people to hold the meeting, a quorum, according to the regulations. When he or she is satisfied that there are at least the regulation number of people present, the meeting is opened. The chairman welcomes those attending and states the purpose of the meeting. He or she may also read through the agenda, or, if members have a copy, may simply refer to it as the running order.

The chairman then calls on the secretary to read the minutes of the previous meeting, and when this is complete asks whether the people present agree that the minutes are a faithful record of that meeting. When the minutes are agreed, the chairman signs them. After they are signed, the chairman asks if there are any questions or matters arising from the minutes of the last meeting, before asking the secretary to read any correspondence that has a bearing on the current meeting – mostly apologies for absence.

Finally, the business of the meeting can get under way. When the meeting is finished, the chairman announces the date and place of the next meeting and closes.

Informal meetings

The vast majority of meetings are informal. They may be meetings between a client and supplier firm, or between members of different departments. Informal meetings are not bound by the same rigid legal rules that bind formal meetings, but the chairman still needs to be in command in an effort to see fair play and to get something done.

As with formal meetings, it is the chairman's business to ensure that the right people attend, and that all the relevant information is circulated beforehand if necessary. During the meeting, unfettered by the formal structure of motion, amendment and voting, the chairman must be able to identify and sum up the issues arising out of the discussion, and to ensure that some sort of conclusion arises (even if it is the conclusion that no conclusion is possible!). After the meeting, he or she should also circulate notes of the meeting, with details of the action(s) agreed upon.

Because the chairman of an informal meeting has the power to direct it, it is much more tempting to become involved in the discussion. However, it is still vital that you avoid this so that you retain the power to control and guide the meeting towards a suitable conclusion.

KEY POINTS

√ remain polite and impartial
√ understand the rules and enforce them
√ transact business quickly and efficiently
√ be firm and fair

ROLES AND EVENTS

CHAIRPERSON'S SPEECH TO COMPANY AGM

Every company in the UK is required under the law to hold an annual general meeting to announce the year's profits, share dividends and other figures, and to seek ratification from the shareholders of those decisions that cannot by law be made by the board alone.

Chairperson's duties

Whether your company holds its AGM in the room above a local pub, or hires a venue such as London's Albert Hall, it is customary before the business is begun, for the chairperson to make a speech.

Use this opportunity to congratulate members of the company in general for a good performance last year. Even if times have been hard and the company did not perform as well as expected, try to be optimistic and to point out some successes, however small.

Enumerate some of the changes that have taken place over the last year, and show how they will be of benefit. If yours is a small company, it may be appropriate to welcome new employees, or lament the loss (perhaps through death) of old employees.

You may wish to say something about the state of the industry in general, and perhaps to place your company in that context. How are you doing against age-old competitors? Has your market share increased? Is the industry contracting or expanding?

Look to the future. Tell shareholders (in general) the changes that you wish to make, and why you wish to make them. Alternatively, mention changes that have already been instituted that may soon start to show benefits. Be optimistic in your outlook, but not unrealistic – shareholders are likely to withdraw their support if you seem to have your head in the clouds.

If you are the chairperson of a small company, and perhaps you have never given an address like this before, you may find inspiration in the annual reports of other companies (you will find these in a business library, or you might persuade a company to send you a copy). These normally begin with 'a few words from the chairman', and will tell you the kinds of things you could include in your speech.

While this is not a time for levity, you may wish to tell a humorous anecdote (perhaps related to scandals in the industry), in order to break the ice. On the whole, though, appear business-like and serious – your shareholders have money at stake and they would probably not be too impressed to find that they have entrusted it to a comedian.

Keep it brief. Avoid making long lists of last year's events (pick out only the most successful) and don't blind the audience with complicated figures. The rest of the meeting may well turn out to be long and arduous, so don't make matters worse.

Remember to welcome the shareholders and to thank them for their continued support and interest.

KEY POINTS

✓ **keep it short**
✓ **be optimistic but not unrealistic**

See Also:
Chairing a Meeting

CHRISTENINGS

Speeches in honour of the newborn usually take place at christening parties in the form of a toast, proposed either by one of the godparents or by a senior member of the family, for example a grandparent.

Just as the aim of a christening or infant baptism is to welcome a newborn child into the Church, so a christening speech should aim at welcoming the child into the family as a whole. The speaker should therefore represent all the family.

Compliment the mother and father on their child, and welcome the godparents. If you are yourself one of the godparents, you might say that you consider it an honour to have been chosen. It is usually also customary to point out that the child has a good start in life, and that the parents should prove more than equal to the task of bringing up the child.

You might like to use an anecdote about one of the parents, or you might chose a quotation that fits the bill. Whatever you do, though, avoid getting into family disputes or opening old wounds. This is a time for celebration and family unity, not strife.

KEY POINTS

√ welcome the child and its godparents into the family
√ avoid family disputes
√ be positive about the child's future

Don't forget to thank those who have organized the christening party, and don't forget to toast the baby!

A reply, if there is one, should come from one of the parents, thanking the family on behalf of themselves and the child.

CONFERENCES AND CONVENTIONS

To the outsider it sometimes seems that business people, academics, scientists, politicians and the clergy take every opportunity to leave their desks to attend a conference or convention. Those not in a position to attend themselves, might see such events as a dreadful waste of time, but well-organized conferences and conventions are a golden opportunity to improve communications, pass on information and raise the profile of one's activities or products.

Speeches

Speaking to a conference or convention is similar to lecturing (**Lectures** p.194). The major difference is that the audience is likely to be made up of experts like yourself rather than of mixed level or predominantly lay. While this means that you may be at liberty to go into fine technical detail, there is no excuse for a stultifying speech. Furthermore, as the conference progresses, audiences may start to suffer from battle fatigue, and you will

---

EXPERT-TO-EXPERT

If you don't check and double-check your facts and figures, you put your professional integrity at risk. More than in any other speaking situation, you are likely to be found out and called to account. Don't risk it!

---

therefore have to fight all the harder for their attention and appreciation.

The kind of speech you make at a conference obviously depends on the purpose and context of the gathering. Find out all the details from the organizers before you begin to plan your speech (see **Accepting an Invitation to Speak** p.1).

You may be there to sell your product or idea to colleagues in your industry. Therefore you must bring to bear all your persuasive skills (but be careful – if you are a salesperson talking to salespeople, they will know all the tricks too, so be subtle and genuine!).

Alternatively, you may have been invited in order to pass on information, so aim to do just that – spend time structuring your speech to be informative and memorable. Use visual aids if you believe they will increase understanding, and tell the audience why they should spend time listening to you rather than sloping off to the bar.

Keeping their interest

If you are lucky enough to be speaking on the first day of a conference, you will probably be honoured with a capacity audience made up of intent listeners. However, you may be billed to speak at less advantageous times: after lunch when everybody is sleepy; early in the morning when some might have hangovers; late in the afternoon when people are thinking about evening jaunts; on the last day when most people are sick to the back teeth of the subject in question and are contemplating the long drive home. At these times, the audience will be less than attentive.

Check the time at which you are expected to speak, and be aware that you will have to work harder to enthuse your audience and help them retain facts. You may even be able to turn a last day slot into a triumph. Being among the last, your speech is likely to be the one speech that delegates will remember the most clearly.

Using your time
When you are not speaking, use your time to listen to other speakers. This is not only polite (if you expect to be listened to, you must listen to others in your turn), but it will also give you some idea of the ways of the audience. They may have a bawdy or subtle sense of humour; they may be reluctant questioners; they may (heaven forbid) harbour hecklers. Use this intelligence to ensure that your speech will go down well with the audience. Learn from other people's mistakes and successes.

When no speeches are scheduled, socialize with other delegates. This way you can continue your intelligence gathering. Also, if members of the audience know in advance that you are likeable, interesting and interested, you have laid the ground for a warm reception when your turn to speak arrives.

Don't try out parts of your speech on other delegates, but if you find that you are listening to an anecdote that may prove illuminating if you retold it from the platform, ask for permission, and do so. The person who told it to you will be flattered, and you will show that you are interested in what other people have to say.

Reading your speech
Find out whether you are expected to supply a paper beforehand and then deliver it verbatim. If so, you may need to find a way to deliver it so that the live audience does not doze off, or simply up and leave (see **Successful Delivery** p.67).

Conventions and conferences – checklist
Research and prepare your conference speech as you would any

other full-length presentation. Here is a checklist of some of the more important points to remember in the run-up to the big day:

- Have you written and delivered material for the chairperson to use when introducing you?
- Have you double-checked the details of when and where you are expected to make your appearance?
- Have you checked that you have your notes and visual aids with you?
- Have you double-checked personal arrangements such as hotel accommodation, travel, fees and expenses?
- Have you checked out the conditions at the venue?

On the day:
- Check that your visual aids are in position and that all necessary equipment is working.
- Check the venue. Make sure that the air conditioning is working to your advantage. Check also for possible distractions.
- Ask a steward to shepherd the audience into a compact group at the front and centre of the room, the better to make eye contact with them and to mould their group responses.
- Clear the room of odds and ends left by other speakers – paper cups, used flip charts – anything that will distract attention.

For speakers and audiences alike, conferences and conventions can be an enjoyable and efficient way to communicate with other members of a profession, industry or interest-group. Capitalize on this opportunity to raise awareness of your work, product or thinking, to learn from other speakers and to discover the interests of other people in your field.

KEY POINTS

√ take this golden opportunity to communicate
√ check and double-check your facts
√ check arrangements with the organizers
√ prepare to combat flagging interest
√ gather intelligence wherever you can
√ learn from the mistakes and successes of others

See Also:
Business Meetings
Business Presentations

DEBATING

Many people leave it until later in life to gain experience of speaking in public. Why wait so long? Many schools and universities run debating competitions and clubs, which enable young people to learn the valuable skills of putting together an argument and impromptu speaking. Even if you never had this opportunity (or passed it up) in youth, debating is a vigorous and entertaining way to get some practise now.

Competitive debating

This is closely associated with parliamentary debating, in which the Government argues the point with the Opposition, presided over by the Speaker of the House, and the outcome is decided by voting. So it is clear that sharply-honed debating skills are vital to political life.

In competitive debating, two teams, usually of three people each, are pitted against each other, under the guidance of a chairperson. A judge awards marks to each member of the team, thereby reaching a decision as to which team has managed to expound the best argument. A motion is drawn up, for example – 'This house believes that the age of chivalry is dead', or 'This house believes that religion is the opiate of the masses'. One team is asked to speak for the motion and the other speaks against.

Starting with the first speaker for the motion, each team member takes a turn in this order: first speaker for; first speaker against; second speaker for, and so on.

The aim is for each team to try to refute the arguments of the other and establish their own arguments in their place. In this

175

scheme, each team member has a specific job to do, within a certain time limit.

First speaker for

The first speaker for the motion introduces the motion to the house. She must define all the words in the motion and interpret its meaning. Next, she must tell the audience the line of reasoning that the team wishes to take, outlining three aspects that the team wishes to elaborate as the debate progresses. This is rather like any other speaker introducing the topic to be discussed, and outlining the order in which he or she would like to cover each of the sub-topics (see **Planning and Writing**, Structuring a speech p.37).

She goes on to elaborate on one of these segments, leaving the other two for the next speakers for the motion. She ends by summing up the argument so far.

First speaker against

Next up is the first speaker from the opposing team, who has the job of agreeing or disagreeing with the definition set up by the other team (known as the proposition). If he disagrees, then he must set up his own definition and argue the case for having it adopted. If the first speaker against fails to demolish the propositions' definition and interpretation of the motion then that interpretation stands.

He goes on to show that the line of argument taken for the proposition is erroneous and establish his own team's line in its place. Just as the first speaker has done before him, he then goes on to outline the way in which his team will be developing the argument (once again in three segments) and deals with his part of that development. He then sums up.

Second speaker for

Now the second speaker rises to her feet. She should first of all refute the definition set up by the opposition, and knock down their proposed line of reasoning and the first third of their case. She then goes on to deliver the second segment of the case for the motion. When she has done this, she reviews the argument so far.

The second speaker for is probably the most important speaker in the team, in that she has the first opportunity to destroy the case of the opposition, and she must do this in order for her team to have any chance of winning. At this stage, arguments over the definition and interpretation should have been laid to rest and she should have made a strong attack on the first segment of the opposition's argument.

Second speaker against

The second speaker against begins by reinforcing the opposition's line of argument, refuting in the process that of the proposition. He deals with any points arising from the development of the proposition's argument by the previous speaker and puts his segment of the opposition's case.

Third speaker for and third speaker against

The third members of each team continue the pattern, beginning with an attack on the argument of the previous speaker and going on to discuss the final aspect of their respective arguments.

Summing up – against and for

The first speaker on the opposition side is then invited to sum up on behalf of the opposition, reinforcing all the arguments and refuting those of the other side. He ends by contrasting both sides of the argument and 'proving' that his case is more favourable.

Finally, the first speaker for the proposition rises to her feet to restate the case for the proposition and refute that of the opposition, at the end calling for the house to agree that her definitions, interpretation and line of argument holds more water. She should bring all her powers of persuasion to bear in this final summary, but she must not at this stage introduce any new arguments.

Preparation

Your team must first decide on a definition and interpretation of the motion, and then on a line of argument. The definition must be reasonable (that is, it must make sense), and should enable you to mount a strong argument.

Discuss and decide upon three key aspects of the argument, and allocate one to each speaker for further research. Each of these strands of your argument must be directly relevant to the subject in question (otherwise the other side will find it an easy task to knock them down), and must be ordered to follow on from each other in a logical way. Consider how the other team might argue against your points, and make sure that you pre-empt this.

In preparation, it is also important to think of ways in which the other side might choose to define the motion and develop its own line of argument, and prepare ammunition against them.

Each speech should be constructed with a beginning, a middle and an end, with internal linking passages and linking passages between speeches, along with summaries and appeals. Ensure that every single assertion is backed up by rock-solid evidence that proves the point, and when the speeches are written, check that each member of the team has fulfilled the role expected of him or her. Bring to bear all the tricks you know to make your argument persuasive.

On the day

You may spend a great deal of time and energy researching and writing your speech, but it is all useless unless you are capable of thinking on your feet, and being flexible enough to refute the other side's arguments at a moment's notice.

Ensure that each member of the team is equipped with paper and pen, so that they can jot down counter-arguments to be passed up the line to the appropriate team member as others are speaking. When it is your turn to speak, deal with these counter-arguments first, before going on to give your prepared speech.

Flexibility and quick-thinking really are the watchwords here – you may find that you have to rearrange your prepared arguments completely in the face of totally unexpected definitions or arguments.

KEY POINTS

✓ aim to refute the opposing side's arguments and establish yours in their place
✓ be prepared for all eventualities
✓ back up assertions with facts
✓ make sure that your arguments cannot easily be refuted, otherwise, don't waste your breath, throw them out
✓ listen carefully and make notes
✓ be prepared to think on your feet

The essence of debate is reasoned conflict. Deal with every single point energetically and emphatically.

ROLES AND EVENTS

Make your reasoning clear and show that what you are saying is logical, and your team will carry the day.

See Also:
Impromptu Speaking
Business Meetings

FUNERALS AND MEMORIALS

Probably the most difficult speaking occasion you will ever encounter is a funeral or memorial service. This is not only because you will probably have to contend with your own grief, but also because you will be responsible for voicing the deepest emotions of those around you.

The two occasions may be slightly different. A funeral service is normally more personal and immediate than a memorial, because the grief is still fresh and the people attending are likely to be relatives and close friends. A memorial may take place on an anniversary of a person's death, and may include colleagues and even people who did not know the deceased personally, but who are invited because of their professional or official position.

Funerals

At a funeral, the most important people are the immediate family. Find out what they would like you to say, and comply with their wishes. Just as the last thing said in a speech is the thing most likely to be retained by an audience, so the last words pronounced in memory of the dead will be remembered and treasured. Therefore, keep your speech short, simple, personal and sincere, and aim to convey the essence of the character of the deceased. Do not over-dramatize or declaim.

A possible structure:

- Introduce the occasion. Direct the formal address to the close

ROLES AND EVENTS

family, using their Christian names if appropriate: 'George, Andrew and Paula, good friends and family. We are here today to bid farewell to . . .'

● Describe the deceased, mentioning some good times or endearing qualities; perhaps he or she was a pillar of the community or worked in the Church, and it might be appropriate to mention these things.

● Address sympathy to the family and pledge your support.

● You might like to include a reading, perhaps a favourite passage from the Bible or a poem.

● Sum up with a few choice words, for example, the deceased was much-loved, is greatly missed and will be long remembered with affection.

Never speak ill of the dead – if you cannot find something good to say about him or her, even if it means burying a recent grievance, you should refuse to speak.

Finally, do not allow yourself to be so overcome with emotion that you break down. Never drink before giving your speech, but use breathing exercises to steady your emotions.

In memoriam
A memorial is likely to be less overwhelming than a funeral. It is more of a celebration of the dead person's life and work, but it is still a solemn occasion. The structure above may be adapted to the memorial by adding more anecdotes, which may even be humorous.

Try to strike a balance between portraying the private and the public person, and remember to elaborate your relationship to the deceased.

KEY POINTS

√ make the family your top priority
√ keep it simple – never get carried away with grief or rhetoric
√ never speak ill of the dead
√ be sincere, capture the mood
√ be sober but not dreary

GIFTS AND AWARDS

The giving of gifts and awards is an activity that celebrates the achievements of an individual or group. A work colleague may be retiring after many years' service to the company, or just moving on to a different job. Alternatively, the occasion may be the presentation of an award for outstanding services or successes. Whatever the occasion, the essence is to give a verbal pat on the back, and to receive it with grace and modesty.

Presenting a gift or award

If you have been asked to make a presentation, there must be a good reason. Perhaps you are a close colleague of the outgoing member of staff, or a person of some standing within the industry giving the award. Normally, though, you will have personal knowledge of the recipient. If you do not, you may have to seek information from the organizers as to that person's qualifications, past career, etc.

In your speech, start by introducing the occasion, and perhaps explaining why you in particular have been asked to make the presentation. Spend a little time talking about the recipient: character, demeanour, career, influence on others, etc. Add some depth to your speech by comparing the recipient's professional persona with his or her personal character.

You might tell a humorous anecdote about the recipient, but make sure that it shows him or her up in a good light, and that it does not embarrass. Over-zealous praise will also embarrass most people, and it will ring hollow to the audience, so try to make your comments quietly appreciative rather than emphatically superlative. Sum up and present the gift with a few words of congratulations.

> **Keep the physical presentation of the gift/award until you have finished saying your last words, otherwise they will be lost in the activity. Finish what you are saying, and then hand the object to the recipient. Hold it in your left hand and place it into the recipient's left hand, so that there is no fumbling when you come to shake hands with your right.**

Don't hog the limelight. The day belongs to the recipient, so, like the person who has been asked to introduce a guest speaker, aim to focus attention on the recipient rather than on yourself.

As presenter, you have been chosen to represent the group – your work colleagues, or members of your industry – so be careful that you make this clear in your choice of words. Choose your material carefully, so that it echoes the sentiments of all, rather than concentrating on personal feelings that may be peculiar to you. Try to paint a picture of the recipient that most members of the audience can identify.

Receiving a gift or award
Some recipients are asked to make a speech on the spur of the moment – their retirement party was a surprise, or the result of the awards was a closely-guarded secret until the moment of the announcement. If you think that you might be put in this position, prepare a short speech of thanks.

ROLES AND EVENTS

Begin by thanking the presenter, and extend these thanks to the group as a whole. If you are retiring after many years' service, you might like to reminisce *briefly* about the early days of your career with the company. Alternatively, you could mention the project you worked on that brought you the award.

If you are stuck for something to say, simply search your heart, and identify the emotions you feel. Tell the audience that you feel honoured, proud or touched. We have all watched, stupefied, as some tearful show-business luminary reels off an interminable list of credits. Not only is this tedious, but it is also breaking one of the first rules of good speech-making – involving the audience. It may be appropriate to mention a couple of people who 'have made it all possible', but a list of meaningless names will simply alienate listeners. If you really must mention people who are likely to be unknown to the audience, say what role they played in your immediate success. You might mention the support given you by your spouse, but if it seems likely that few people will recognize him or her, a gesture will serve to point out the person you are talking about.

KEY POINTS

✓ be sincere
✓ remember the audience and make your speech relevant to them
✓ avoid interminable lists
✓ keep it short and to the point
✓ if you are on the receiving end, smile!
✓ try not to be overwhelmed or over modest

Your speech of acceptance should strike a balance somewhere between jubilation and modesty. Smile and look around at the audience before you start to speak. This should give you time to compose your thoughts and find your voice in all that emotion, and it will also enable you to connect with the audience. Show that you think you deserve the prize, and never say that you think you don't, or you may be at risk of having the audience believe you. On the other hand, don't crow, and if appropriate, remember to commiserate with the losers.

Whether you are giving or receiving a gift or award, the touchstone is heartfelt sincerity and involving the audience as much as you can.

See Also:
Impromptu Speaking
School Speech Day

IMPROMPTU SPEAKING

If you are known to be a good speaker, or you are an expert in a certain subject, you may be asked to deliver an impromptu speech. Alternatively, you may be attending a lecture by another speaker, and during question time, he or she calls upon you to give your expert opinion. You may be asked for your views at an inter-departmental meeting. You may wish to give your views at a public meeting, or even be required to keep an audience amused while, backstage, a blown fuse is replaced. The skills of impromptu speaking are invaluable to anyone who wants to make him- or herself heard. Gaining experience of speaking in public, by taking every opportunity to speak on the spur of the moment, means that you will be far more assured when it comes to delivering a prepared speech.

Instant panic
Many people dread being called upon to speak. Some may blush uncontrollably when asked to give their name in an informal seminar, others simply find as they rise reluctantly to their feet that their minds have gone completely blank. If this is the case for you, remember that speaking off-the-cuff has one major advantage – you are forced to **do it now**. Action kills fear, so you should find that you have forgotten your fear in the scramble to think up something to say.

Finding something to say
In many respects this is the same problem you face when working on a prepared speech – and the solutions are basically the same.

The most important question you need to ask yourself is, what do I want to achieve? Do you want to make a point that might persuade the meeting to your way of thinking? Do you want to add information to that already discussed? What would you like the outcome of your speech to be – an action, or a feeling?

The first material component you need is a central thought – a single idea around which you can elaborate. Then you need an example or illustration. Pull from your memory a relevant personal experience or an anecdote. Consider what conclusion you would draw from this anecdote, then decide how to wind up. You may conclude with a request, for instance that the audience gives money to the cause, or that a certain body of information be considered in the discussion. Or you may simply repeat the central thought.

Alternatively, you may have no particular purpose in mind, except to amuse. In this case you might like to talk about the audience, or the occasion. You could also pick up on a remark made by a previous speaker and elaborate, adding the benefit of your own experience, and concluding by agreeing or disagreeing with what was said.

Make use of the tools that are already in your speaking armoury. Make an appeal to the audience (see pp.18–21), to show that what you are going to say is of interest to them. Repeat any information you are giving, so that they remember what you have said. Summarize your argument if it has more than one branch.

If you are an expert of some sort, open by introducing yourself and stating your credentials. This will orientate your audience's thoughts towards the subject you want to raise, and make them more likely to take your information or observations on trust.

Pitfalls

Don't go on too long. If you do, you may find that you lose track of your own argument. You will always help yourself if you aim to keep your speech short. No-one expects you to produce a 30-minute speech on the spur of the moment, even in an emergency. Any organizer who asks you to do this is asking for trouble.

Don't struggle to your feet as if you wish the ground had opened up and swallowed you. Make sure that you appear to be glad of the opportunity to speak. Try to summon up some energy with which to galvanize the audience. They need to have a very good reason to listen to you.

Don't speak too quickly in a desperate attempt to get it over with. Remember to use the correct (or at least a polite) form of address, and then speak slowly and deliberately. This will not only improve your audibility, it will also give you a few more precious seconds with which to find the right words.

Preparing and practising

> It usually takes me more than three weeks to prepare a good
> impromptu speech.
>
> Mark Twain

It may seem a contradiction in terms, but many people anticipate being asked to speak, and prepare a few notes. You should do the same, especially if you are attending a public meeting on an issue that is close to your heart or you are an expert in the subject under discussion. However, this does not mean that you should stick to your notes. It is most likely that you will need to attend to what has gone before and to shape your speech accordingly, using your notes simply as a prompt. For example, you may have prepared yourself to make a point, and find that another speaker has covered it. In this case, you should begin by stating that you agree with what that speaker has said and go on to give your reasons. Your speech is no less valid because the point has already been made. Such flexibility is a central skill – practise it whenever you can.

Student actors are often asked to take part in improvisation games in order to hone their skills. You can do the same with family and friends. One such game is to have a member of the company pass you an object found in the room. It could be anything – a vase, a cushion, a book, a plant. Your task is to speak on a subject related to that object for a certain time – say one minute. Alternatively, write subjects down on slips of paper and have each person in turn improvise a speech on that subject.

Alternatively, also with a group of friends or family members, play the storytelling game. Ask one person to start a story, perhaps suggesting an opening sentence taken from a novel. After a given amount of time, say, one minute, the next person must take up the threads of the story. The last person to speak must finish with a second, previously-agreed sentence.

These two games can be great fun, and they will improve your ability to think on your feet immensely.

KEY POINTS
✓ **be prepared to improvise**
✓ **practise with friends**
✓ **state your objectives**
✓ **resort to your speaking armoury for techniques and inspiration**
✓ **speak slowly**
✓ **keep it short**

KEYNOTE SPEECHES

People of high standing – company chairmen, politicians, celebrities – are sometimes invited to deliver keynote speeches at the opening of events such as conferences, trade exhibitions and festivals. The speech that they deliver encapsulates the essence and aim of the event – hence the name.

Preparing the speech

If you are asked to give a keynote speech, find out as much as you can about the event. If it is a conference or lecture series, find out who the speakers are, and what themes they will be covering. Perhaps it is a sales conference. In which case, find out (if you do not already know) what products are being presented. If it is a trade fair, research the industry and find out what will be going on at the fair. You will be able to get this information from the organizers, and they will also be able to tell you if there is any one theme or aspect of the event that they would like you to emphasize.

• Find out also who the event is aimed at: a small group of company salespeople? members of a particular industry? the general public?

• Formulate a statement of the purpose of the event: to pass on information as in a sales conference? to promote international business relations?

• Start by welcoming everyone to the event, and thanking the organizers for inviting you to deliver the keynote speech. Tell the audience the main theme of the event and give your thoughts. Tell them what the aims of the event are, and why they are important.

● In conclusion, you may like to wish all participants success in their endeavours, and encourage everyone to enjoy the event.

When you have drafted your speech, look over it to check that you have the kind of speech you have been asked to deliver – a keynote speech. Remove everything that is not closely related to the event, and ensure that you have provided some food for thought and set the tenor for the rest of the proceedings. Most of all, check that what you have to say will focus the minds of the participants on the business in hand, and your keynote speech will have done its job.

See Also:
Opening Functions

Practical Techniques –
   Accepting an Invitation to Speak

LECTURES

If you are an expert in your field, or someone who has done or experienced something extraordinary, you may be invited to give a lecture. Lectures fall into several broad categories, such as academic lectures, 'how-to' lectures or hobby-related lectures. Lecture audiences also take a wide variety of forms, from school and college students to luncheon clubs, or hobby and social clubs to academic institutions. Wherever you are lecturing and however the audience is comprised, you are expected to supply information and give food for thought. Fail to do this and you will not get very far on the lecture circuit.

The golden rule on lecturing, therefore, is know your field and check your facts. A lecture is a full-scale speech, and should be carefully constructed and rehearsed along the lines described in the section on Practical Techniques.

Know your audience

You will remember that an entire chapter is devoted to this, but some of the main points are worth repeating here:

- Find out from the organizers what kind of people are likely to attend.
- Seek out previous speakers to the same audience and get their opinion on the audience.
- Attend one or two other lectures to this same audience. Note what makes them laugh and what seems to interest them.
- Work out the level of the audience. How much are they likely

to know about the subject already? How much technical detail can you go into before they fall asleep or stop understanding? Will you need to explain technical terms to a lay audience?

These kinds of considerations will tell you how you will be able to engage the audience's interest and enthusiasm, and the kind of material you will be able to use.

LAY AUDIENCES

Never be patronizing to a lay audience. If you do not respect your audience, they will not respect you!

Series continuity

You may have been invited to lecture as part of a series. In this case, it is important to find out who else is speaking, and on what subjects. When you come to write your speech, ensure that you link it to the main theme of the series, and that you mention subject areas discussed by other speakers. If you present your speech in a vacuum, listeners will begin to wonder what relevance your speech has to the rest of the series, so tell them, and give them good reasons to listen.

Using visual aids

Many lectures are enlivened by the use of visual aids, and they can also help to make the audience understand quickly the concepts you are discussing. (See **Visual Aids** p.59).

ROLES AND EVENTS

Titles and introductions

Much stress has been laid on knowing how the audience is going to be constituted, and where their interests lie. However, you may find yourself with no audience at all if you do not enable the organizers to advertise your lecture in a way that attracts interest. As soon as you have decided which aspect of your subject you would like to speak on, formulate a title and let the organizers have it so that they can make a start on advance publicity.

Equally, once you have attracted an audience to a venue, they are going to want to know a little more about you before you begin. The chair of the gathering will be expected to give a short introduction, but don't leave its compilation to him or her. Write the introduction yourself, and make sure that it is received by the organizers in advance. The introduction sets the stage for you, and if you make yourself sound boring or pompous, the audience will show little enthusiasm as you mount the podium. So work hard to produce an introduction that is modest and lively.

Taking questions

It is quite likely that after you have finished your lecture you will be expected to answer questions. This is not an exercise in speaker-bashing! It will give you an opportunity to enlarge on some of the things you have said, or repeat them for greater clarity, but it will also give you a greater insight into the interests of the audience. This is invaluable information, especially if you intend to give your speech again. (See **On The Day** p.104)

Turning professional

Life on the lecture circuit may seem to be an ideal way to make a living – touring the country (or even the world), talking to like-minded people about a subject close to your heart, but as with many professions, only the best succeed. Public speaking as a profession is highly competitive, and you must be able to offer something that is different and valuable to audiences. Turning professional also has its responsibilities: you will be expected to make a good job of it every time (no excuses – people have paid good money to hear you speak).

However, if you are an expert in a subject that interests people, and you have had enough public speaking experience to be able to guarantee that you can deliver the goods, by all means try to get on the circuit. Contact an agency and ask that they take you on (they may wish to audition you or send someone to hear you speak). Alternatively, offer your services to local associations. It is unlikely that you will make a good living out of the lecture circuit, and so, at least at the outset, consider lecturing as a supplement to other work.

Whether you are professional or amateur, lecturing can be a very enjoyable activity. You will meet a wide range of people, and you will have the satisfaction of passing on your enthusiasms to others.

KEY POINTS

√ be expert
√ research your audience
√ give them what they expect
√ write an engaging title and introduction

See Also:
After-dinner Speaking
Conferences and Conventions
Slide Shows

MEETING THE PRESS

Now more than ever, it seems that press coverage is central to getting your message across, whether you are a business person, a charity organizer or political campaigner. Even academics now have to come down from their ivory towers to speak to the press in an effort to raise the profile of their work (and so guarantee finance).

There are two circumstances in which you might find yourself talking to the public through the media: first, in interviews or panel discussions that are designed for broadcast on radio or television (see Radio and Television p.217); second, at a press conference where a number of print journalists are present, or in a pre-arranged one-to-one interview.

Press conferences

A press conference is called when a person or organization wishes to release a statement to the press. It is usually arranged by a professional press officer or PR consultant. Once members of the press have arrived, a statement will be made, and afterwards questions are often invited. The wording of a press statement should be worked out in advance, and it should always be read word for word.

Reading a statement is the easy part. Handling questions effectively requires a cool head and some quick thinking. Discuss with your press officer beforehand the kinds of questions that are likely to arise, and work out how best to respond. Decide also how much you want to elaborate on the statement, and the kinds of things you want to say. Decide how long you wish to remain in the line of fire, and make sure that your press officer is present on the day to chair the conference and draw it to a close.

Taking questions – dos and don'ts

- Do remain standing while taking questions, to maintain your dominant position and for good audibility.
- Do listen carefully to each question and think before you speak.
- Do try to read between the lines, to discover what the questioner is really getting at.
- Don't enter into arguments or bow to personal abuse.
- Do rely on the conference chairperson to chose questioners.
- Do refuse to answer questions that you believe to be unfair or irrelevant.
- If you don't know the answer to a question, admit it rather than trying to bluff your way through.
- Don't be drawn into commenting upon unsubstantiated facts.
- Don't be negative – always speak in positive terms: question – 'Has the police investigation come to a dead end?' answer – 'No, the police still have many more leads to follow up' is better than 'The investigation has not come to a dead end'.
- Don't lose your temper.
- Do keep your sense of humour.
- Do remain courteous at all times.

One-to-one

Interviews are an entirely different kettle of fish. They are normally conducted one-to-one, with a tape recorder running. Tell the journalist beforehand how much time you are prepared to spend on the interview, and bring it to a close when the time is up.

Find out beforehand what the journalist wants to talk about

and research the publication. Work out what that publication's interest in your story might be, and how they are likely to present it to their readers (see below). Try to anticipate questions so that you can formulate appropriate answers.

Keep your answers short but informative. Don't be drawn into disclosing information unintentionally (answer the question put, and don't volunteer extra information unless you have to). Beware of making hasty statements.

Don't treat the journalist as an enemy. She may ask some searching questions, and it may seem to you as if she is attacking you. This is most often not the case. She is simply trying to put herself in her readers' shoes so that she can elicit from you the information they would be interested to read, and ask the questions they would like to ask.

A good journalist will ask you 'open' questions, that demand that you elaborate rather than giving a simple 'yes' or 'no' in response. Remember, though, that every statement made by the journalist on which you comment could be quoted as yours, so if you want to qualify your agreement or disagreement, do so.

Off the record

Every word you say in an interview, even a flip comment uttered when the journalist has said goodbye and is heading for the door, is 'on the record' (liable to be quoted), unless you expressly tell the journalist that you would like to go off the record. When you do so, the journalist should switch off the tape recorder, or put aside the notebook. Interviewees go off the record in order to tell a journalist something that he or she should know in order to understand what is being discussed, but that they do not wish to have repeated or attributed to them. If a journalist has this information substantiated on the record by two or more other people, however, he or she is likely to publish (but is still not allowed to connect the information with your name). Strictly, you are off the record until you indicate that you wish to go back on the record.

Avoiding misrepresentation

The ways of the press are mysterious. Many people are wary of coming into contact with journalists because they feel that they will be deliberately misrepresented. This is very rarely the case.

The main job of a journalist is to find a story that will draw the attention of his or her editor and readers. This means that any information you present at a press conference or in interview will be angled to suit the readership and the publication concerned, just as you would put a different slant on an anecdote to tailor it to the interest of your audience.

Because of this, you may find in some instances that the main point of what you were saying has been lost in what seems to you to be a debris of apparent trivialities. In worse cases, journalists get the wrong end of the stick completely, and you may find that you have been grossly misrepresented through genuine misunderstanding.

In a very few instances, journalists deliberately set out to present you and your message in a bad light. If you can prove this, then you have every right to redress either through the Press Complaints Commission or through the courts.

It is your job to communicate your message clearly, leaving as little room as possible for misunderstanding. Equally, if you want to reduce the possibility of journalists concentrating on a lesser part of your message, or representing it in a newsworthy but inappropriate way, it is up to you to control them.

The best way to do this is to give journalists what they want – a good, topical story that will interest their readers. Work with your press officer to formulate your message in a way that satisfies both your needs and those of the publication(s) in question.

ROLES AND EVENTS

> ### KEY POINTS
> √ do your homework
> √ stay in control
> √ put your message across clearly
> √ never be drawn into making rash statements
> √ think before you speak

See Also:
Impromptu Speaking

Practical Techniques –
  On the Day: Question time, p.114.

OPENING FUNCTIONS

Fetes and bazaars, buildings, parks, shopping centres, exhibitions and trade fairs. These are some of the occasions at which you might be asked to give an opening speech. You may be invited to do so for a variety of reasons. You may be the mayor, or some council or government official. You may be a patron or worker involved with the beneficiary charity. You may be the president of the company or trade association.

Whatever the reason, and whatever the occasion, always aim to keep it brief. On most occasions, the audience will be standing, rather than sitting down, and it is likely that they will have a great deal to distract their attention. At charity events such as fetes and bazaars, there might be very young children present, who are not normally inclined to stand still and listen. Four or five minutes is quite long enough.

Being heard

It is often the case that you will be either speaking outdoors or addressing people scattered across a wider than normal area, and therefore the chances are that you will need to use some form of public address system.

Whatever equipment you are faced with (and this can vary between a loud-hailer and a full-scale sound system), make sure that you have time to check it before you begin to speak. Talk to the organizers and make sure that the system has been set up so that people in all parts of the venue can hear properly. You may have to test it yourself, and if this is the case, enlist someone to tell you whether you can be heard at the extremes of the venue. Call the organizers a few days in advance, and ask what system is going to be used, then practise.

Remember to speak slowly so that you can be understood, especially if the system generates a time-delay between speakers, or the venue gives back an echo.

Being seen

At some functions of this kind, you will find that you are surrounded by people who are all standing. It may, therefore, be difficult for people to see you. If you think that this is the case, ask the organizers to find something on which you can stand so that you can be seen by as many people as possible.

Ensure that people do not crowd too closely around you, making it difficult for you to be seen and heard. On the other hand, you may find that your audience is scattered across a wide area, with huge gaps between the different groups of people. Ask the organizers to act as stewards to round up the audience.

Background research

You will need to find out what the occasion is, and why you have been asked to attend. If the event is in aid of a charity, and you are not already involved, find out about their aims and work. The same goes for a company.

At this stage, you may need to decide whether you agree with the charity or company's aims. Even if you are not directly involved, you will be associated in people's minds with the organization. It is up to you to decide whether or not this is a good thing. For example, a person who considers conservation important may not wish to be associated with a chemicals producer seemingly intent on polluting the local estuary!

Find out who is going to be introducing you – make sure that you get their name right, and that you know how to pronounce it. Equally, find out if there is anyone who has been central in organizing the function, or making the completion of the project possible.

Content

Start by thanking the introducer and those who have invited you to open the function. Go on to say how pleased you are to be able to attend. If you have a special interest in the project or charity, say so.

You may need to talk about the project and the people who have made it possible, or to mention the beneficiary charity. The point here is to give reasons why it is important that the event is taking place. Be concise. Say why the project/charity is a good idea and draw a picture of the people who will benefit. Try to relate this to the interests of your audience (see **Appeals and fund-raising speeches** p.134).

If you are opening an exhibition, say something about the exhibits and the exhibitors. If you are opening a trade fair, you may say something about the companies that are attending, the success of the previous year's fair, or some of the changes taking place in the industry as a whole and relate that to the purpose of the fair.

Make time to thank the organizers of the event for putting in so much time and effort to make the whole thing possible. Mention them by name if you can, but if there are too many to list (and this is extremely tedious for outsiders), you could use the formula, 'Mrs Jones and the members of the Church Committee/Julie Campbell and her team from marketing.' Try not to step on anybody's toes by missing them out – but do remember your time limit.

In winding up your speech, encourage people to take part in the function: to part with their money in a good cause; to enjoy the attractions; to look round the building; to have a successful trade fair. Then declare the function open.

This basic structure can be varied with the use of short quotations or anecdotes. You may wish to make a generalization based on statistics or other information, particularly if you are opening a business– or industry-related function.

Remember, however, to keep it short and relevant to the occasion.

Avoid using the platform to score political points or to put across dogmatic opinions. Your role is to celebrate the opening, not start an argument or ruffle people's feathers. If you feel that you cannot perform this function without making your personal or political views known, then perhaps you should not accept the invitation.

Finally, don't simply step down from the platform and make for the nearest exit. Take time to look around at least part of the function, and speak to some of the people involved – they are part of your audience as well as the guests who have been invited to attend.

KEY POINTS
√ keep it brief and make it relevant
√ give praise where praise is due
√ celebrate the opening
√ don't make political points or air your personal opinions

See Also
Keynote Speeches

PANEL DISCUSSIONS

Panel discussions could be seen as a form of controlled seminar, at which the audience is given the opportunity to question panellists on a defined subject area or range of subjects. Some panel discussions, for example, for television and radio broadcast, may concentrate on current affairs, with the occasional 'personal' question thrown in, whereas others, particularly at conferences, centre on a single field. In the latter case, panellists are sometimes asked to give a brief presentation of views or information to focus the questions.

Preparation and planning

You may be asked to join a panel for two reasons. You may be an expert in the field under discussion, or you may be a person in the public eye – a politician or celebrity. Whoever you are, it is more than likely that you will be asked to send the organizers some information to be used in the chairman's introduction of you to the audience. Make sure that you do this in good time – difficulties may arise if you are misrepresented.

If you have been asked to make a presentation, prepare it as you would any other speech. When it comes to questions, however, you will need to use all your skills as an impromptu speaker. It is therefore vital that you prepare yourself thoroughly, so that you can give well-formulated answers. Try to answer the following questions:

- Will the questions be general (current affairs), or will they be centred on a particular subject?
- If there is a defined subject for discussion, what is it?

ROLES AND EVENTS

- Are you expected to give a résumé of your views or provide information, as a starting point?
- Why have you been asked to join the panel?
- Who are the other panellists? What are the reasons for their inclusion?

When you have the answers to these questions (and you may have to make a phone call to the organizers in order to get them), you will be able to anticipate the kinds of questions you are likely to be faced with, and the sorts of views that are likely to be put forward by the other panelists in response.

Decide what your standpoint is. Make some notes, and if you think you will need further (perhaps statistical) information to back up your arguments, do some research. Consider arguments for and against. Try to work out whether you are going to be able to count on allies on the panel, and who, if anyone, you are likely to be arguing against.

On the spot

Here are some hints for a successful panel discussion:

- Always take a pen and some paper with you (these should be provided by the organizer, but it is better to be safe than sorry).
- Write down the name of the questioner, and the question. Make some notes on your response, and if you have time, quickly organize them into a coherent statement with a beginning, middle and end. Don't scribble furiously – a quick list of key words should be enough to act as a prompt.
- If you want to give some statistics to back up your answer, don't make it too obvious that you are reading them – the audience wants to believe that they are putting you on the spot, not that you have prepared your arguments in advance.

- Never whisper to your neighbour while a question is being put, or, indeed, while another panellist is speaking.
- If you are still formulating your answer (or stuck for inspiration) when the chairperson asks for your answer, ask him or her to come back to you. If you are in dire straits you may find that one of the other panellists says something with which you can agree and on which you can elaborate.
- Always begin your answer by saying that you agree or disagree with what one of the other panellists has said, and then elaborate. This provides continuity in the discussion.
- Try to direct the start of your answer to the questioner, and perhaps use their name. But do not speak to him or her exclusively (or the chairperson or other panellists). Open up your range of eye contact to include the whole company.
- Try not to be agreeable all the time. The audience will enjoy the occasion more if there is dispute and debate, rather than bland agreement on all sides.
- Avoid slander.
- Never relax! Listen intently to what others are saying, and choose your words carefully. Never resort to aggressive argument.

KEY POINTS

√ **do your homework, be prepared**
√ **anticipate likely questions and possible differences of opinion**
√ **stay relaxed**
√ **encourage debate, but don't lose your cool.**

ROLES AND EVENTS

See Also:
Impromptu Speaking

**Practical Techniques –
  Accepting an Invitation**

POLITICAL SPEECHES

**From Cicero to Churchill and beyond, political
speech-making has been at the centre of the art of
rhetoric. Skilled speakers down the ages have been
made famous by their ability to sway the masses.
Nowadays, senior politicians more often than not
employ speech-writers who are well-versed in the
tricks of the trade. At all levels, political
campaigns are co-ordinated by professionals to
present a unified front to the voting public.**

Political objectives

The public will judge a politician by his or her promises and
evidence of ability to fulfil such promises. However, which
promises will win an individual's vote, and what constitutes evidence to a voter, varies from one person to the next. In a political
campaign each party tries to establish its political priorities as
those of the country (or region) as a whole, and to show that its
candidates are honest enough to represent the will of the people
and smart enough to make decisions on behalf of the country as a
whole. At the same time, each party will try, by fair means or
foul, to undermine in the eyes of the public the policies and
candidates of the other.

   You are therefore in the business of persuading the audience
that you will act in their best interest and that the other candidate will not. You must defend yourself against the 'attacks' that
the other party makes on your policies and attack those of the
other party yourself. You must also provide the public with
memorable phrases so that they associate you with a particular
action or issue and with a bit of luck, remember your name when
the time comes to vote.

ROLES AND EVENTS

Know the audience

The most important tenet to keep in mind when putting together a political speech at any level is that the audience wants something from you. In this case, they come not only with general subconscious needs (see **Knowing Your Audience** p.15), but with specific political issues in mind: the future of local hospitals; the efficiency of the education system; security of local jobs and industries; the right of women to abortion; the eradication of racism.

Each speech in a campaign is different, because at each venue the audience is different. Find out what the issues are that are most likely to be exercising the audience. Canvas local opinion. Find out what people want and show that you are the person to give it to them. If they want something different to what your party wants, it may be your task to persuade them that they want something else!

Find out how the members of your audience lead their lives and what their aspirations are. They may be predominantly middle-income executives whose priorities may be good trading conditions for local businesses and improved schooling for their children. They may be miners or car workers. You may be confronted with an audience of students or shopkeepers. Speak to your audience about the issues that are most important to them,

---

A HELPING HAND

It is unlikely that you will be campaigning alone. You will have the support of your local party, and you should be able to call upon their campaign expertise. You may even be given the services of a professional speech-writer.

---

in language that they understand. No-one wants to be represented by a person who has no grasp on their own brand of reality, so you must show that you do understand the audience's concerns and that you are committed to addressing them.

Cut and thrust

Like it or not, when involved in a political campaign, it is just as vital to discredit the opposition as to establish your own credibility in a similar way as in a debating contest you would attack the opposing team's arguments while seeking support for your own.

Personal attacks are a last resort. The public tend to consider them dirty tactics and think less of you as a result. Reserve your attacks for a candidate's policies. You are at liberty to shred the opposition's policies – indeed this is what political campaigning is (or should be) all about, the public scrutiny of arguments and standpoints leading to a majority consensus.

However, it is possible to build on a personal failing that the public is beginning to pick up on and apply that failing to that candidate's policies. A candidate may appear in public dishevelled and badly dressed. You might therefore say that his policies are in a shambles, that they are disorderly and muddled, that they have been thrown together in a hurry. A candidate may appear too slick, and public opinion may consider her an intellectual who is too clever by half. Her policies could therefore be attacked for having no grounding in reality, irrelevant, unrealistic, or misguided. Alternatively, your opponent may have made a few blunders and a couple of U-turns, and so the emerging concensus is that he is unsure. Build on this by applying terms such as confused, unbalanced, inconsistent, inconstant, wavering, irresolute.

Use the thesaurus to build up an amoury of synonyms that consolidate the picture you want to paint. Don't use them in a long list, but apply one or two during each stage of your attack.

ROLES AND EVENTS

Let them do the work for you, little by little transferring the audience's subjective impression of the candidate as a person to his or her policies.

Another good way to make an attack on the opposition without seeming to do so and therefore losing the respect of the public, is to attack sideways. Your opponent has been accused in a local newspaper of small-time fraud. Mention the subject by saying that you will not mention it. By refusing to comment, you have put yourself across as someone who is above such things.

Shield-work

If you are in the business to attack your opponent, however subtly you may do it, you will need to defend yourself against incoming fire. There are two things to remember here. First, never use the negative terms of your opponents. If you have been called a liar, it would do more damage than good to state 'I am not a liar' – the term sticks, whether you are a liar or not. Say instead, 'I have always been honest in my dealings with the public...'

Second, do not avoid uncomfortable issues or attacks. Deal with them immediately and get them out of the way. Aim to spend as much time as possible in your speech on the positive issues without ignoring or glossing over the negative.

> **It is best to avoid humour as far as you can. Just like the company chairman who insists on cracking jokes for the benefit of shareholders at the AGM, very few people will entrust their political futures to a comedian.**

Sound-bites

In these days of media campaigning, it is vital that your message is media-friendly. Give your audience a memorable message and the press something to use in their headlines. This skill comes down to the words you use and the ways in which you string them together. If you can produce a well-turned and catchy phrase, that appeals to the public's imagination, the press will use it, and this can only be to your advantage.

Find famous quotations and proverbs that you can manipulate. Use alliteration and rhythm to make a sentence or phrase punchy. Most of all find ways of saying things that are vivid and evocative.

On the platform

Political speech-making is not for the faint-hearted. You are quite likely to be heckled in the time-honoured fashion and you will probably face hostile questioners. Don't betray your nerves, but learn to respond quickly and decisively. Hesitation can be construed as a sign of uncertainty. Thorough preparation can see you through most of the fray, but only practise and a cool head can ensure that you emerge without a scratch.

KEY POINTS

√ establish your priorities
√ demolish those of the opponent
√ never make personal attacks
√ never avoid the negative
√ emphasize the positive
√ speak to be remembered and reported
√ respond decisively to hecklers and questions

ROLES AND EVENTS

Finally, arrange your speech so that you save your strongest and most important arguments and your most evocative sound-bites for the finish.

See Also
Debates
Impromptu Speaking

Practical Techniques –
   Knowing your Audience
   Improving your Style

RADIO AND TELEVISION

The broadcast media are the most powerful tools of communication at the speaker's disposal. Radio and television could transmit your message to millions of listeners and viewers. Both mediums require the speaker to master particular skills in order to be able to send the right message.

Different requirements

Radio broadcasts put you across as a disembodied voice. The way you look is immaterial, and this may be an advantage to some. On the other hand, you will need to pay special attention to the way your voice sounds, and because your listeners cannot see illustrative hand movements, you must work harder to paint evocative pictures with your words.

By contrast, television not only allows the viewer to see you, it also has the disadvantage of amplifying defects. You must therefore work hard at presenting a palatable image while still making sure that what you say makes sense and is heard above the visual 'distraction'.

Preparation

Just as you would when anticipating an interview with a print journalist, it is essential to ask questions when you are invited to take part in a radio or television broadcast:

- What is the programme?
- What is the issue under discussion?
- Why are you being asked to take part?
- What is the editorial policy of the programme (is there any bias in their reporting or treatment of the subject in hand)?

ROLES AND EVENTS

● Who are the other interviewees (if any)? Contact them and find out what their views are.
● What is the programme's target audience, and what is their interest in your story?
● What kinds of questions will be asked?
● Is the programme to be broadcast live?

Define for yourself a number of points that you would like to make – not too many, broadcast interviews are normally very short indeed. Write down these points and think of a way in which you might be able to illustrate each one. You should be able to make each of your points in short concise sentences. If you need to explain in detail you had better find something else to say – you will inevitably be cut off by a broadcaster with one eye on the clock.

Try to find out if you can what kind of introduction you will be given. Check the facts and correct them if you know them to be untrue or biased. Find out what the first question is going to be – knowing that at least should give you some comfort at the outset when your nerves are bound to be jangling the loudest.

In the studio
When you enter a studio for the first time, you are bound to be bewildered by all the paraphernalia. Ignore it. Listen carefully to instructions and try to stay relaxed – extreme nerves show up in the voice and will be spotted on your furrowed brow or in your body language. If you can, have a look round the studio before you go on air, just to make yourself at home, though this is not always possible.

Voice control for radio
When answering questions on radio, speak at normal volume, as if you were having a conversation. Take care to breathe nor-

mally. If you are nervous you may become breathless, or your voice will waver. Make every effort to control this. Because you can't be seen, you will be able to use a cue card or crib sheet, but avoid rustling papers.

Body language for television

Good television technique comes with experience. But the home video camera now provides a very useful way to practise before your first appearance, if you have the time and the resources. Record your rehearsals and compare your appearance and mannerisms with those of people you see on television every night.

Get used to making yourself comfortable in the hot seat. Ensure that your body is balanced but that you are not so relaxed as to be slouched into its deepest recesses. Put your hands in your lap and leave them there. Keep them away from your head and face at all costs and don't fiddle.

Never look at the camera. Keep your eyes on the interviewer and speak only to him or her. Make your face expressive – this is where the camera will be concentrating – but not too expressive. Concentration can often show on the face as a frown, which can easily be interpreted as anger. Equally, nerves can be transformed into a fixed smile, which can be interpreted that you have something to hide or that you are being flippant about a subject that you should take more seriously. Try looking solemn if discussing unhappy or serious subjects, and smile when being optimistic. Make your face a tool to emphasize the meaning of your words. Practise with a video camera or in the mirror.

Avoid moving too much, without looking as if rigor mortis has set in. If you make sudden large movements, the camera operator will have great difficulty keeping you in shot, and the effects can be quite startling.

ROLES AND EVENTS

Speaking beyond the interviewer

For both television and radio it is important to remember that you are speaking to an audience of millions rather than to a single person. The presence of a studio audience should help, but make sure that you remember the need to explain yourself to others rather than taking it for granted that the audience knows what you mean because the interviewer does. A good broadcaster will ask questions as if he or she were one of these unseen millions, allowing you to put your message across in a coherent and interesting manner.

Answering questions

The basic rule for answering questions for television or radio broadcast are the same as for any other question and answer session: listen carefully to the question, and answer it in a few words. A good question (an open question) should enable you to amplify your answer somewhat to add interest. Therefore, avoid plain yes or no, but keep your answers to a couple of sentences for the sake of time.

It may appear that given the direction the questions are taking, you will not get a chance to state your key points. If this is the case you may need to take control of the interview. Don't be rude or stubborn – answer the question put to you quickly and then go on to reorientate the interview in the direction you want.

Nobody likes to see or hear interviewees refusing to answer questions. If there is a subject that you do not want brought up on air, tell the interviewer or researcher beforehand. Get agreement that the subject will not be touched upon. If it is mentioned during the interview, simply say that there is an agreement not to go into that area because it is beside the point/not relevant/counter-productive/etc. If you have to do this, make sure you remain agreeable and reasonable rather than becoming petulant.

Speaking on radio or television does not always take the form of the arranged interview or panel discussion. You may be stopped in the street and asked to give your opinions on a particular subject, or you may be asked to comment over the telephone on an event or issue. You may voluntarily call in to a 'phone-in', goaded into airing your views by being forced to listen to those of others. On another level, your company may decide to make use of video for advertising, selling or training purposes, and you may be asked to take part. However you become involved, the broadcast media are such powerful means of mass communication that it would be foolish for anyone who regularly speaks in public to overlook them.

KEY POINTS
√ do the background research
√ prepare key statements and illustrations
√ stay in control of your voice or body
√ practise any way you can
√ speak to the wider audience
√ answer the question but take control if you have to

See Also:
Impromptu Speaking
Meeting the Press
Political Speeches

Practical Techniques –
  Improving your Style
  Successful Delivery
  On the Day

SCHOOL SPEECH DAY OR PRIZE-GIVING

School pupils make a deceptive audience. The audience at a school speech day is likely to be made up of children and young people of ages ranging from 12 or so to 18, as well as their adult teachers. This is a classic mixed-level audience, and so you must pitch your speaking style accordingly.

Correct approach

While it is necessary to keep your ideas and the words you use simple, be careful not to patronize the audience. Never refer to them as 'children'. Even if you consider them to be so, they do not believe that they are, and they will quickly turn against you if they perceive you to be talking down to them. On the other hand, do not to be too 'modern' in your language or casual in your appearance. Dress as you would normally dress to be smart, and as far as is consistent with audience understanding, use the words you would use in normal conversation.

The concentration spans of young people are even shorter than those of adults. Therefore keep your speech short – five or ten minutes is quite enough – and use all the techniques you know to keep them interested.

Material

You will probably find that the majority of your material will come from your own experience. Think back to speech days when you were at school – were you bored? Were there any humorous disasters that you can relate? Do you have any anecdotes from your school days, or can you poach one from someone else? Perhaps you were a mediocre student and never won a prize – describe your feelings (remember, however, that you have probably been invited to honour prize-winning students, so avoid belittling their achievements). Perhaps you remember an unbearably long speech made while you were a student, and this will almost certainly mean something to the audience! Choose one anecdote only, draw a conclusion, and make that your central thought.

The humour of the young is very different to that of those of us who are older. If in doubt as to whether the audience will be amused by a joke, try it out on your own or someone else's children first.

Congratulate the winners

Remember the occasion. You have probably been invited to give out prizes and to join in a celebration of the achievements of the school. While it is probably not your task to list the school's successes (the head will probably do this), you should remember to congratulate the prize-winners at the start or end of your speech.

If you are the person who is giving out prizes, congratulate each student – a simple 'well done' or 'congratulations' is enough. Try to show that you are interested in each individual student – stay alert and smile. At intervals, you may like to say

---

KEY POINTS
√ avoid patronizing children
√ keep it short, simple and relevant
√ be interesting and interested
√ congratulate the winners and encourage the others

---

more to a particular student – to pass a comment ('Well done – I always came bottom at Latin when I was at school.'), or to ask a question ('Will you be going on to university next year?') – to show your interest. However, organizers will want to get through this part of the proceedings as quickly as possible, so avoid having a full-scale conversation.

SEMINARS AND WORKSHOPS

The seminar or workshop format is now widely used to train or to brief many different groups of people, from employees to charity volunteers. All have a defined aim, and include a wide range of teaching and discussion techniques for use in small groups. Some seminars take place in the course of a single day, while others can continue over a weekend or a week.

Seminar leaders

The key player at such an event is the group leader. While he or she may not be the person who put together the material, devised the exercises, or structured the event, the ability of the group leader to elicit a suitable response from the group, and to push the discussion process forward to the proposed end is vital. For both the leader and the participants, impromptu speaking is a necessary skill.

As a seminar leader, you may well not be writing your own material. Instead, it is likely that you are presented with a 'curriculum' which you must follow. While you may not have to put together your own speeches, there are a number of things that you can do to make the event thought-provoking enough to elicit the necessary discussion among the group members, and to ensure that the discussion runs along the expected lines.

Your position as the seminar leader is very important. Rather like a person chairing a meeting, it is important to gain and maintain the respect of the participants, while still facilitating open discussion.

Always give more time over to listening than to talking. Make sure that you seem attentive, and that you are willing to countenance almost any contribution. Do not, however, countenance discourtesy among participants, or be discourteous yourself. If one participant threatens to disrupt the flow of the proceedings, be polite but firm. Point out that while what they are saying is interesting, you will be covering it in the afternoon session, or it is drawing the conversation away from the point. If one particular person is being disruptive or discourteous, take them aside during a break and explain to them that they are causing a problem. If a group discussion is becoming heated, you might also wish to make the point to the group that you require courtesy from everyone.

If you are worried about whether a particular exercise will be successful, never allow the participants in on your secret. Most role-playing games and exercises rely on the participants' willingness to go along with you. If you announce that you have never tried this exercise before and you have your doubts as to whether it will work, some people may take it as licence to spend their time criticizing the structure of the exercise, rather than trying to make it a success. Do not dismiss criticisms of your performance or of the activities that you have set up. Listen to them, and take them seriously, but try to move on as fast as courtesy allows.

Watch your body language. Because seminars present some of the most informal of speaking situations, you may be tempted to relax too much. By all means enjoy yourself, and encourage the group to do so as well, but remember that you need to stay in control. Whether you are leading a discussion or giving a keynote presentation, stand up. Make eye contact with the participants. If you do so, you will have their attention, but you will also be more likely to notice when somebody wants to say something. When asking for contributions, stand still, and let your gaze wander around the room. Do your best to appear friendly and open.

Keep your notes and other paraphernalia tidy. Clear up after one session in preparation for the next.

As with all forms of public speaking, the key to leading a seminar is control tempered with flexibility.

Getting to know you

It is nine o'clock on the first day, and you are faced with a number of new faces. You do not know the seminar participants, and they do not know you or each other. You are anxious about how the day/weekend/week will go, and nervous about saying your first words. The participants are likely to be just as nervous as you are. They may have no idea what to expect, and many of them are not looking forward to talking in front of the group.

You may try to break the ice with a naming session. Ask each person to introduce themselves, and to say a little about who they are, where they come from, what they do for a living, anything relevant. Alternatively, ask the group to divide into pairs, and to introduce themselves to their neighbours, and then ask the neighbour to introduce their partner to the group.

Another method of having people introduce themselves, and to break down the barriers between people, is to ask them to answer a list of questions about how they are feeling:

- What is your name?
- How do you feel when you meet new people?
- What do you do when you walk into a room full of strangers?
- What do you do when you are nervous?

Again, it helps to have people go through such questions with a partner before they are asked to do so in front of the group. Variations on this method lead to a more personal response, and may not be suitable for strictly professional, teaching occasions.

Some of the best teachers and seminar leaders have taught

themselves the trick of learning peoples' names in a very short space of time. Try to do the same, and to use names whenever possible. If the seminar requires a high level of ease among the participants, urge them to follow your example – you might even promise a prize to the person who can name all members of the group within a certain time.

Defining the structure

It is important at the outset to run through the agenda for the seminar, just as you would include in the opening of an ordinary speech a list of the points you wanted to cover (see **Planning and Writing** p.32). This enables the participants to see the progression that they are expected to make under your guidance, and the kinds of things they will be asked to think about.

At the start of each session, recap on the issues discussed in the previous session and go on to announce the session title, and to give some idea of the kinds of things that you will be wanting to discuss. This is the same process as linking one part of the argument together with another when structuring a speech. Equally, every time you move from one phase of the discussion to another – perhaps to an exercise or some other activity, announce that you are moving on.

If the seminar extends over a number of days, it is important to recap on the previous day's activities. An evening spent at the hotel bar may have clouded the participants' recollections of the previous day's work, and it is desirable for continuity that you remind them.

When presenting participants with an activity or exercise, give clear instructions. Ask whether the instructions have been understood, and if necessary (and appropriate), describe the kind of outcome you are expecting.

Brainstorming

Brainstorming is a useful way to open a discussion. Ask a question that requires a list of answers. Use a blackboard, whiteboard or flip chart to write down the answers in a list. Take as many of the answers as you can, even if they are not relevant at this stage. Ask for clarification of a response that is not concise enough.

You should have some idea of the kinds of answers you will get, and you should be prepared during the brainstorming session to ask questions that will draw the right answers.

When you have come to the end of the suggestions, run through them and try to group them together. If this is not possible, run through them to recap. You might then ask participants to elaborate on their suggestions or to draw conclusions from the list.

Maintaining interest

Many seminars and courses pack a lot in to a very short time. Be aware, therefore, that participants may lapse into fatigue at certain times – early mornings, after lunch and at the end of the day are the most likely times. It might be a good idea to schedule activities for these times, rather than bland discussions during which people will inevitably switch off.

Speak to the participants' own interest and experience. You may find that your group is made up of people with diverse professional backgrounds. Find out what these are during naming sessions or in conversation during breaks. Remember them and if possible, call upon their professional experience to illustrate or reinforce a point – most people are more at ease speaking authoritatively as experts than as individuals. Feel free to retell suitable anecdotes or to make points made by members of the group during breaks – people will be flattered that what they have to say is remembered and considered important enough to relate to the group.

ROLES AND EVENTS

Getting a response

If you are having trouble eliciting a response, use the techniques you would use to add interest to a speech – draw from your own personal experience and ask others if they have encountered the same or similar situations. Ask for a response:

- Has anybody found themselves in the same situation?
- What did you do?
- Has anybody used this software system?
- Did you encounter any problems? What were they? How did you solve them?

It may be that participants do not follow your train of thought, or understand your question. Restate the question in different terms, or suggest a possible answer and ask for someone to agree with you and elaborate.

If the response you are getting is confused, say the answer back to the participant, and ask them if that is what they meant. Try to interpret what they are saying to the group as a whole, and if necessary move from the specific back to the general. Ask whether other people believe that your generalizations are fair and logical.

Using visual aids

Visual aids can be put to good use in the seminar situation. Flip charts can be used to record the results of brainstorming sessions, and to note a progression in the group's discussion. Pages can be torn out and stuck to walls to remind group members of the work that they have done. Videos can be used to give information and to illustrate and make progress. Handouts can be useful for activities or to sum up a process that has been under discussion.

Make sure that you are not using too many visual aids. While it is possible to usefully combine more types of aid in seminar situations than in other kinds of speeches, a great deal of time can be wasted moving people from one room to another, or getting organized in other ways. See **Visual Aids** p.59)

Participating in seminars

The seminar or workshop is an ideal place for you to practise your speaking skills. You may be terrified when asked to introduce yourself to the group, but this should subside as the course goes on and you become more at ease with your fellows.

It goes without saying that you should try to be attentive to the discussion and to be as active as you can without hogging the limelight. Look out for the leader's clues as to what the session is about, and what its purpose is. Try to stick to the point.

In discussion, follow the suggestions for impromptu speaking. If you have nothing to add to what has already been said, agree with someone who has already spoken and repeat their point. Perhaps on the way you may find you can elaborate and enlarge on it. Call for agreement from other members of the group.

Make your point clearly and slowly. You might think of an anecdote to illustrate it. Draw a conclusion to bring the discussion back to the subject in question. You may find it useful to make notes so that you can remember which point you wanted to pick up on.

Do not become involved in heated arguments. If you disagree with someone, say so, and back up your opinion with good reasons.

Try to be co-operative with the group leader. Even if you are attending involuntarily, remember that, if nothing else, this is a good opportunity to practise your own speaking skills in a relaxed environment, and perhaps also to learn from some good speakers.

As the seminar continues, you should feel more relaxed. Your nerves should subside and you will find it easier to express yourself. As your co-participants become friends, rather than strangers, beware of relaxing too much. Remember that you are attending this seminar for a reason, and keep in mind what that reason is.

KEY POINTS

Leaders
√ **stay in control**
√ **explain instructions clearly**
√ **use recaps and summaries**
√ **draw on your own and other people's experience to enliven discussion**

Participants
√ **stick to the point**
√ **remember the aims of the seminar or workshop**

See Also:
Chairing a Meeting
Impromptu Speaking

SLIDE SHOWS

Many lectures or talks are greatly enhanced by the use of slides. Even if the entire event is structured around your pictures (say, of your recent trip to the Himalayas), it is important that you construct what you have to say in the same way as any other speech.

Checklist

● Find out what the set-up is:

– Will there be a projectionist? If so, you may need to make a copy of the full script with cues written in. (See **Successful Delivery** p.67)

– Will you be able to operate the projector, and does the set-up enable you to do this without turning your back on the audience?

– Will you be speaking from a podium/lectern, and if so does it have (a) a light to illuminate your face and notes, and (b) a mirror so that you can check the screen without turning round?

● Whether you are working from a full script or just notes, note down each slide, so that you can check that you have the right slide on the screen at any given moment.

● Make sure that at all times your slides are directly relevant to what you are saying, rather than just a vague illustration. You should not have to break off from your train of thought to give a 'caption'.

ROLES AND EVENTS

• Check that your slides can be seen – avoid making up title slides with print that is too small or using weak colours.

• Check that all your slides are of high quality – poor lighting or badly-focused pictures look amateurish.

• Avoid turning to look at a slide. If you must do so, avoid doing it while you are speaking.

• Do not try to show too many slides – allow time for the audience to take in and understand what they are seeing.

KEY POINTS

√ check the set-up in advance
√ annotate your script or notes with details of the slides
√ check that your slides are relevant to your argument

See Also:
Practical Techniques –
  Visual Aids

SPEAKING TO A FOREIGN AUDIENCE

Few people are born to be multilinguists, and even if you find it easy to pick up enough of a language to survive and perhaps hold a simple conversation, giving a speech in a foreign language is likely to be a daunting prospect – a prospect that increases daily with the growing imperative to encourage foreign trade. However, make your position clear to the organizers, and put in a little extra preparation, and you may still come away with another success under your belt.

A 'common language'

You may be asked to speak to an audience that shares English as a first language, but don't be lulled into a false sense of security. Whoever said that Britain and the USA are two countries divided by a common language was right, and the same goes for any other English-speaking nation. Therefore, make sure that you are using understandable idioms. You may even exploit the use of your audience's idioms to humorous effect – British accent pronouncing a typically American phrase can be very endearing, and may help to break the ice.

Whenever you are speaking to a foreign audience, try to show that you have some knowledge of their country and culture. Include references to current events (from newspapers and magazines) or local activities (especially sports).

ROLES AND EVENTS

Speech-making in a foreign language

It may turn out that you simply cannot get away without making your speech in the local language. You may be blessed with the ability to do this, but unless you are completely confident of your fluency, it is best to have your script professionally translated. It is probably a good idea also to take some coaching – ask a national to attend one of your rehearsals, to check that you are not making unforgivable mistakes.

Working with an interpreter

If your audience does not speak English (and you do not speak the local language), and you need to get across exactly the right message – perhaps you are presenting complex figures to a client company, or making a potentially sensitive political speech – then you would do well to work through an interpreter.

When working in this way, deliver your speech as you would normally, but make sure that you speak slowly and that you leave pauses at the ends of phrases or sentences. Each unit of speech should make sense in its own right, but it should not be so long that by the end, the interpreter forgets where you started!

This process can be very laborious, so endeavour to keep your speech as short as possible.

JOKES

Many jokes lose something in translation. British humour in particular is notoriously difficult for many foreigners to understand, as it often depends on British idioms that are a mystery to foreigners.

Using English

When talking to the organizers, you may find that the audience will be able to understand what you are saying if you deliver your speech in English. If you plan to do this, it is a good idea to have your opening remarks translated for you so that you can be seen to be making an effort, even if it is simply to apologise for needing to revert to English for the rest of your speech. Try to approximate the accent of the region – you might ask friends or the organizers to spend a little time coaching you.

Toasts to foreign hosts or guests

In some countries, for example, many Asian countries, it is customary for hosts and guests to toast each other at the end of a meal. If you have been invited to a meal ask a national for advice on etiquette. For business entertaining overseas, it might be appropriate to propose a toast to the host/guest company, or to a particular leading member of the other side's delegation. You might also propose a toast to the success of future, joint ventures. Whatever the occasion, make sure that you take advice, not only on the theme for your toast, but also on mealtime manners and customs.

KEY POINTS
√ communicate with the organizers
√ make an effort to be understood
√ practise makes perfect
√ ask a native speaker to coach you, even if you think you are fluent

---

WEDDING ANNIVERSARIES

Like a christening speech, that at the celebration of a wedding anniversary (most often the silver and gold – 25 and 50 years respectively) takes the form of a toast, usually proposed by the couple's oldest friend. If you find that you are expected to hand over a gift, see Gifts and Awards, p.184.

When looking around for a good quotation or anecdote to use in your speech, you may find it difficult to come up with one that is pro-marriage! If you do have trouble, consider shocking your audience by using an anti-marriage quotation, and then announce the couple as living proof that the quotation was wrong.

These days, no-one really believes that marriage is a bed of roses. Avoid, therefore, painting an overly sentimental picture of unwavering romantic love. The close friends and family gathered for the occasion are more than likely to know that the couple has experienced the ups and downs of life – what you are here to celebrate is the fact that, however they managed it, their marriage has survived.

You might raise some laughs by mentioning habits that have been a minor bone of contention between the couple, but don't mention any well-kept secrets. Try to paint a picture of the couple that is recognizable, plausible and pleasing.

Life-stories

Consider a couple of anecdotes about 'the early days', which will be of interest to younger members of the family and a source of nostalgia to contemporaries of the couple. Avoid giving a lengthy life-story (you are, after all, merely relating events that everybody should already know of), but if you think it is interesting, sketch out the shape of the couple's married life and pick out one or two 'landmarks': the birth of children and grand-children, moving house, successes, recoveries from illness.

End by looking forward to the future and wishing the couple well for the coming years. Ask the company to add their congratulations and to drink a toast to the couple.

Replying to the toast

The reply is made by one of the couple, usually the husband, and is begun by thanking the proposer of the toast and the assembled family and friends for the good wishes.

The central part of the reply should be directed towards your spouse. This is a golden opportunity to say how much you have appreciated his or her company all these years, and to offer thanks for their love and support. Whatever words you find to say this, make it heartfelt and you will not go wrong.

KEY POINTS

✓ **don't give away any secrets**
✓ **don't be sweetly sentimental**
✓ **be sincere**

WEDDINGS

For many people, weddings are the only time in their lives when they will be asked to give a speech. Wedding speeches are most often given by novices who suffer from nerves and self-doubt. Yet this is one of the most important days in the life of the newlyweds (if this is not their first or last marriage, it is at least the only occasion when they will marry each other), and so it is crucial that you put up a good show.

The form

It is customary to have three speeches, and all are toasts. The first toast is proposed by the bride's father, or a close family friend or relative. He or she proposes the health of the bride and groom. Next, the groom replies, and proposes a toast to the bridesmaids. Finally, the best man replies on behalf of the bridesmaids. At some weddings these days, women have begun to assert themselves. Occasionally, the bride will rise after the groom has finished, to give a short speech of thanks. Alternatively, best men are sometimes asked to share the limelight with best women, and sometimes, the opening speech by the bride's father is dropped altogether.

While some people disapprove of these modern changes in custom, there is one advantage in such flexibility. If the father of the bride really cannot face speaking in public, and refuses point blank to do so, at least the bride and groom are able to let him off the hook and invite someone who will make a good job of it.

Each of these speeches should be prepared in advance and delivered as one would deliver any other long speech (see the

Practical Techniques section). The following are suggestions as to how to generate material for each speech.

The bride and groom

The toast to the bride and groom should express happiness at the occasion and wish them both luck in their new life. It is customary to compliment the bride on her appearance and congratulate the groom on his luck. You may be able to draw an affectionate (though not embarrassing) anecdote from having known the bride for so long, or you may have a funny story to tell about the first time you met the groom. Alternatively, you may wish to pass on some words of wisdom about the nature of marriage, and the qualities a couple need to succeed (but try to avoid being pompous). Finish by asking the guests to raise their glasses and drink to the health of the bride and groom.

WEDDING-SPEECH DON'TS

- **Never make the bride or her mother the butt of a joke.**
- **Never make remarks in bad taste.**
- **Avoid smut, innuendo and references to past partners.**
- **Don't make in-jokes that only one person will understand.**
- **Don't use the opportunity to score points in family disputes.**
- **Remember that this is the bride's special day, and only add to her pleasure.**

ROLES AND EVENTS

The bridesmaids

Next up is the groom, who thanks the proposer of the previous toast (if there is one) and in turn proposes the toast to the bridesmaids. It is usual that this speech begins 'My wife and I ...' eliciting a round of applause at his first use of the phrase.

The groom usually compliments the bride on her appearance and thanks her for consenting to marry him. He usually also comments on his good fortune at having found her. He thanks his best man for supporting him, and for working so hard to ensure that the day has run smoothly. Sometimes, the groom also thanks the bride's family for allowing him the honour of marrying her, but this is something else often frowned upon by brides – ask her how she feels about it first! Even if he does not thank the bride's family for the 'gift' of the bride, the groom should at least thank them for accepting him into their home as a son.

Having discharged most of his duties, the groom is now free to tell a couple of anecdotes (perhaps about how he met his future wife, or something endearing that she did when he proposed) and maybe a joke or two (especially at the expense of the best man), before he turns to the subject of the bridesmaids. He should compliment them on how well turned-out they are, and

---

MIXED-LEVEL AUDIENCES

When preparing a wedding speech, remember that you are addressing a mixed audience. There may be several generations present, so make sure that your comments will appeal, and be understood, by everyone. Most importantly, never offend any one group or class of people who might be present.

---

thank them for attending his wife so ably. He finishes by proposing a toast to the bridesmaids.

The main event

The best man's speech is usually anticipated as the highlight of the occasion. The audience is expecting to laugh, and to be let into a couple of harmless secrets. The best man's speech is usually the longest, but no more than about five to ten minutes.

Start by thanking the groom on behalf of the bridesmaids. Add your compliments to both them and to the bride.

The usual course of events after this is to say something about your relationship with the groom, and to recount some lively stories of your youth together. While it is expected that you will embarrass the groom slightly, it is important that he retains his reputation intact.

Best man's humour

Don't allow your speech to turn into a string of jokes, just for the sake of getting laughs. Dot your speech with a few quips, and if one of them does not go down too well, strike similar gags off your list.

Never make jokes in bad taste, and censor your anecdotes. Remember there may be older people present whose sensibili-

---

WARNING

Alcohol and speech-making do not go together, otherwise you may find yourself carried away by the combination of nervous adrenaline and alcohol. Until you have done your duty, consider one drink the limit.

---

ties you may offend. Avoid lewd comments about wedding nights and honeymoons.

At the end of your speech, read any telegrams or other communications of good wishes, and introduce any special guests: those who have travelled an especially long distance to attend the wedding, for instance. Keep this business section short – the audience is probably by now becoming not so much festive as restive.

Other speeches

If the bride and groom decide that they want to vary this format, they should tell everyone involved and work out who is going to propose which toast.

If the bride wishes to make a speech, she usually takes the opportunity to propose a toast to the people who have helped to make the wedding such a special occasion.

While you are quite at liberty to arrange for as many speeches as you wish, avoid allowing them to go on too long. Immobility, alcohol and large quantities of food, topped off with the drone of seemingly endless orators is enough to put even the bride to sleep!

KEY POINTS

√ make sure that the best man co-ordinates
the speeches
√ avoid remarks and jokes in bad taste
√ keep it short and upbeat
√ be complimentary and good-humoured
√ relate your speech to the audience

Celebrate!

After all the hard work you have put in to prepare your speech, don't forget that a wedding is a time of convivial celebration. Try to show people that you are enjoying the honour of speaking on this occasion, and most especially, work hard to communicate your happiness to your audience.

See Also:
After-dinner Speaking

APPENDIX I
FORMS OF ADDRESS

All formal occasions demand that speakers address their speeches to the audience, starting with special guests. Some people consider this protocol outmoded and unnecessary in today's supposedly egalitarian society, but the custom still exists and should be observed, however far you choose to go in your adherence to the rules. To fail to acknowledge honoured guests, or to use the incorrect form of address can cause embarrassment to the host and may insult the guest in question, and it will probably set you off on the wrong foot. If in any doubt at all as to what form of address to use, ask the toastmaster, an aide, or the organizers.

The basic principle is to acknowledge the special members of the audience roughly in order of importance, using their formal titles, and including any person to whom you are replying. Unless royalty is present, always list the chair of the meeting first. Of course, if there is more than one member of the peerage present, you can cover them all with 'My Lords, Ladies and Gentlemen'.

Make sure all the important people are listed, that you have checked their names, and that you know how to pronounce them.

The following is a guide to the forms of address used when speaking before those with titles. The list runs in order of precedence within each group and shows three forms: the style for the formal address, to be used at the opening; the form for an introduction, if you would like specifically to introduce and welcome a person; the style for a reference, to be used each time you mention a specific person after the introduction.

ADDRESS	INTRODUCTION	REFERENCE
ROYALTY		
King/Queen		
Your Majesty	Her Majesty the Queen	Her Majesty
Note: the Queen Mother is also addressed in this form		
Prince		
Your Royal Highness	Full title: e.g. His Royal Highness, Prince Philip, Duke of Edinburgh	His Royal Highness
Princess		
Your Royal Highness	As for PRINCE	Her Royal Highness
PEERS, BARONETS & KNIGHTS		
Duke		
My Lord Duke, or Your Grace	The Duke of [place]	The Duke
Duchess		
Your Grace	The Duchess of [place]	The Duchess

ADDRESS	INTRODUCTION	REFERENCE
Duke's daughter My Lady	Lady [Christian name + family name]	Lady [Christian name]
Duke's younger son My Lord	Lord [Christian name + family name]	Lord [Christian name]
Marquis My Lord	The Marquis of [place]	Lord [place]
Marchioness My Lady	The Marchioness of [place]	Lady [place]
Marquis's daughter My Lady	Lady [Christian name + family name]	Lady [Christian name]
Marquis's younger son My Lord	Lord [Christian name + family name]	Lord [Christian name]

ADDRESS	INTRODUCTION	REFERENCE
Earl My Lord	The Earl of [place]	Lord [place]
Countess My Lady	The Countess of [place]	Lady [place]
Earl's daughter My Lady	Lady [Christian name + family name]	Lady [Christian name]
Earl's younger son Mr [Family name]	Mr [Christian name + family name]	Mr [family name]

Note: the eldest son of a Duke, an Earl and a Marquis takes a courtesy title. No child of a peer below the rank of Earl takes a title.

Viscount My Lord	Viscount [place]	Lord [place]

ADDRESS	INTRODUCTION	REFERENCE
Viscountess My Lady	Viscountess [place]	Lady [place]
Baron My Lord	Lord [place]	Lord [place]
Baroness My Lady	Lady [place]	Lady [place]
Baronet My Lord	Sir [Christian name + family name]	Sir [Christian name]
Baronet's wife My Lady	Lady [Christian name + family name]	Lady [Family name]
Knight Sir [Christian name]	Sir [Christian name + family name]	Sir [Christian name]

ADDRESS	INTRODUCTION	REFERENCE
Knight's wife		
Lady [family name]	Lady [family name]	Lady [family name]
Dame		
Dame [Christian name]	Dame [Christian name + family name]	Dame [Christian name]
Government		
Prime Minister		
Mr/Madam Prime Minister	The Prime Minister, Mr/Mrs [full name]	The Prime Minister
Cabinet Minister		
Minister	The Right Honourable [full name]	The Minister
Clergy		
The Pope		
Your Holiness	His Holiness the Pope	His Holiness

ADDRESS	INTRODUCTION	REFERENCE
Archbishop (Church of England)		
The Archbishop of [place name]	Archbishop	Archbishop
(Roman Catholic)		
His Grace the Archbishop of [place name]	Your Grace or Archbishop	Your Grace or Archbishop
Moderator		
Moderator	The Moderator	The Moderator
Cardinal		
Your Eminence	The Cardinal	The Cardinal
Bishop (Church of England)		
The Bishop of [place name]	Bishop	Bishop
(Roman Catholic)		
His Lordship Bishop [surname] of [place name]	My Lord	My Lord

ADDRESS	INTRODUCTION	REFERENCE
Chief Rabbi Chief Rabbi	The Chief Rabbi	The Chief Rabbi
Dean Dean	The Dean	The Dean
Provost Provost	The Provost	The Provost
Archdeacon Archdeacon	The Archdeacon	The Archdeacon
Provincial Father Provincial	The Father Provincial	The Father Provincial
Canon Canon	Canon [family name]	Canon [family name]

ADDRESS	INTRODUCTION	REFERENCE
Monsignor Monsignor	Monsignor [family name]	Monsignor [family name]
Prependary Prebendary	Prebendary [family name]	Prebendary [family name]
Vicar/Rector Vicar/Rector	Reverend Mr [family name]	the Vicar/rector
Priest Father [Christian name or family name]	Father [full name]	Father [Christian name or family name]
Rabbi Rabbi/Dr [family name]	Rabbi/Dr [full name]	Rabbi/Dr [family name]

ADDRESS	INTRODUCTION	REFERENCE
Minister Mr/Dr [family name]	Mr/Dr [full name]	Mr/Dr [family name]
Diplomatic Ambassador Your Excellency	His/Her Excellency, the [place] Ambassador	His/Her Excellency
Minister Minister, or Mr [family name]	The Minister	The Minister
Chargé d'affaires Chargé d'affaires, or Excellency (courtesy title only)	Chargé d'affaires	The Chargé d'affaires

ADDRESS	INTRODUCTION	REFERENCE
Academic		
University Chancellor		
Mr/Madam Chancellor	Chancellor [full name]	The Chancellor
Vice-Chancellor		
Mr/Madam Vice-Chancellor	Vice-Chancellor [full name]	The Vice-Chancellor
Professor		
Professor [family name]	Professor [full name]	The Professor
Legal		
Lord High Chancellor		
Lord Chancellor	The Lord Chancellor	The Lord Chancellor
Lord Chief Justice		
My Lord Chief Justice	Lord [family name]	Lord [family name]

ADDRESS	INTRODUCTION	REFERENCE
Master of the Rolls My Lord Master of the Rolls	Lord [family name]	Lord [family name]
Civic **Lord Mayor** Your Worship, or My Lord Mayor	His Worship the Mayor	the Lord Mayor
Lady Mayoress My Lady Mayoress	Lady Mayoress	the Lady Mayoress
Mayor (of city or borough) Mr/Madam Mayor	The Mayor	the Mayor
Councillor Councillor	Councillor [family name]	Councillor [family name]

ADDRESS	INTRODUCTION	REFERENCE

Chair

Mr/Madam Chairman

If the chair is a person of rank, use their title: e.g. 'My Lady/Lord Chairman'.

If the chair happens to be an official, use his or her title: 'Mr/Madam President, ladies and gentlemen'.

APPENDIX II
USEFUL QUOTATIONS

> Next to being witty yourself, the best thing
> is being able to quote another's wit.
> Christian N. Bovee

Every experienced public speaker has in his or her armoury a host of weapons with which to interest the audience. One of these is the ability to find an apt and amusing quotation to fit the occasion.

The following selection of quotations is not designed to replace a full-scale dictionary of quotations, but to act as a foundation for a personal collection. Some are humorous, whereas others are thought-provoking. They can be used as illustrations, as the subject of debate, or to set the speaker off on a particular train of thought.

The quotations have been selected for their relevance to common speaking situations. They are arranged by subject under the following headings:

Art, literature and music
Education and knowledge
Friends and enemies
Food and drink
The human race
Journalism and the media
Justice and law
Life and death
Love and marriage
Parents, children and families
Politics, politicians and power
Religion

Science
Speech-making
Sport and leisure
Travel, exploration and places
Virtues and vices
War and peace
Women and men
Work, business and money.

Art, literature and music

I have been told that Wagner's music is better than it sounds.
Mark Twain

A musicologist is a man who can read music but can't hear it.
Sir Thomas Beecham

Literature is mostly about having sex and not much about children; life is the other way round.
David Lodge, *The British Museum is Falling Down*.

All writing is garbage.
Antonin Artaud, *Selected Writings*.

Literature is news that STAYS news.
Ezra Pound, *ABC of Reading*.

No man but a blockhead ever wrote, except for money.
Samuel Johnson, Boswell's *Life*.

Style and structure are the essence of a book; great ideas are hogwash.
Vladimir Nabokov

A highbrow is the kind of person who looks at a sausage and thinks of Picasso.
Sir A.P. Herbert, 'The Highbrow'.

APPENDIX II

Every time I paint a portrait I lose a friend.
John Singer Sargent

He has Van Gogh's ear for music.
Orson Welles

Music is essentially useless, as life is.
George Santayana, *Little Essays*.

Good painters imitate nature, bad ones vomit it.
Miguel de Cervantes, *El Licenciado Vidriera*.

Education and knowledge
The further one goes, the less one knows.
Lao-tze, *Tao Te Ching*.

When you educate a man you educate an individual; when you educate a woman you educate a whole family.
Charles D. McIver

Try to learn something about everything and everything about something.
Thomas Henry Huxley, memorial stone.

Men must be born free; they cannot be born wise, and it is the duty of any university to make free men wise.
Adlai Stevenson

If you think education is expensive – try ignorance.
Derek Bok

Genius does what it must, and Talent does what it can.
Owen Meredith, Lord Lytton, 'Last Words of a Sensitive Second-Rate Poet'.

Examinations are formidable even to the best prepared, for the greatest fool may ask more than the wisest man can answer.

Charles Colton, *Lacon.*

Oxford gave the world marmalade and a manner, Cambridge science and a sausage.
Anon

An expert is a man who has made all the mistakes which can be made in a very narrow field.
Niels Bohr

If the Romans had been obliged to learn Latin they would never have found time to conquer the world.
Heinrich Heine

Friends and enemies
What is a friend? A single soul dwelling in two bodies.
Aristotle

The belongings of friends are common.
Aristotle

Hell is other people.
Jean-Paul Sartre, *Huis Clos.*

A man cannot be too careful in the choice of his enemies.
Oscar Wilde, *Lady Windermere's Fan.*

I count myself nothing else so happy
As in a soul remembering my good friends.
William Shakespeare, *Richard II.*

True happiness
Consists not in the multitude of friends,
But in the worth and choice.
Ben Jonson, *Cynthia's Revels.*

Friends are God's apology for relatives.
Hugh Kingsmill

APPENDIX II

Old friends are the best. King James used to call for his old shoes; for they were easiest for his feet.
John Selden, *Table Talk*.

Old friends are the great blessing of one's later years – half a word conveys one's meaning.
Horace Walpole

When your friend holds you affectionately by both hands you are safe, for you can watch both his.
Ambrose Bierce

Food and drink
The discovery of a new dish does more for the happiness of man than the discovery of a star.
Anthelme Brillat-Savarin

Conversation is the enemy of good wine and food.
Alfred Hitchcock

A man who exposes himself when he is intoxicated has not the art of getting drunk.
Samuel Johnson

God sends meat and the Devil sends cooks.
English proverb

The best sauce in the world is hunger.
Miguel de Cervantes, *Don Quixote*.

Cookery has become an art, a noble science; cooks are gentlemen.
Robert Burton, *Anatomy of Melancholy*.

After a good dinner one can forgive anybody, even one's own relatives.
Oscar Wilde

We lived for days on nothing but food and water.
W.C. Fields

There is no love sincerer than the love of food.
George Bernard Shaw, *Man and Superman*.

One reason I don't drink is that I want to know when I'm having a good time.
Nancy Astor

Water taken in moderation cannot hurt anybody.
Mark Twain, *Notebook*.

The human race
Mankind is divisible into two great classes: hosts and guests.
Sir Max Beerbohm, *Hosts and Guests*.

The human race, to which so many of my readers belong.
G.K. Chesterton, *The Napoleon of Notting Hill*.

In the future everyone will be famous for fifteen minutes.
Andy Warhol

Man was formed for society.
William Blackstone, *Commentaries on the Laws of England*.

There are but two families in the world as my grandmother used to say, the Haves and the Have-nots.
Miguel de Cervantes, *Don Quixote*.

... the city is not a concrete jungle, it is a human zoo.
Desmond Morris, *The Human Zoo*.

Journalism and the media
I hope we never see the day when a thing is as bad as some of our newspapers make it.
Will Rogers

APPENDIX II

Four hostile newspapers are to be feared more than a thousand bayonets.
Napoleon

Modern journalism ... justifies its own existence by the great Darwinian principle of the survival of the vulgarest.
Oscar Wilde

An editor is one who separates the wheat from the chaff and prints the chaff.
Adlai Stevenson

Journalists say a thing that they know isn't true, in the hope that if they keep on saying it long enough it *will* be true.
Arnold Bennett, *The Title*.

Publish and be damned.
Duke of Wellington

The Price of justice is eternal publicity.
Arnold Bennett, *Things That Have Interested Me*.

Justice and law
In England, justice is open to all, like the Ritz Hotel.
Anon

The Common Law of England has been laboriously built about a mythical figure – the figure of 'The Reasonable Man'.
Sir A.P. Herbert, *Uncommon Law*.

We do not get good laws to restrain bad people. We get good people to restrain bad laws.
G.K. Chesterton, *All Things Considered*.

The law is a ass – a idiot.
Charles Dickens, *Oliver Twist*.

A jury consists of twelve persons chosen to decide who has the better lawyer.
Robert Frost

I don't want a lawyer to tell me what I cannot do; I hire him to tell me how to do what I want to do.
J. Pierpoint Morgan

Ignorance of the law excuses no man; not that all men know the law, but because 'tis an excuse every man will plead, and no man can tell how to confute him.
John Selden, *Table Talk.*

Life and death
It is as natural to die as to be born; and to a little infant, perhaps, the one is as painful as the other.
Francis Bacon

In this world nothing can be said to be certain, except death and taxes.
Benjamin Franklin

Whom the gods love dies young.
Menander, *The Double Deceiver.*

It is better to die on your feet than live on your knees.
Dolores Ibárruri

There is no cure for birth and death save to enjoy the interval.
George Santayana, *Soliloquies in England.*

This world is a comedy to those that think, and a tragedy to those that feel.
Horace Walpole

APPENDIX II

A man dies still if he has done nothing, as one who has done much.
Homer, *Iliad*.

We all labour against our own cure, for death is the cure of all diseases.
Sir Thomas Browne

Death is nothing at all. I have only slipped away into the next room. I am I and you are you. Whatever we were to each other, that we are still . . . What is death but a negligible accident? Why should I be out of mind because I am out of sight? I am waiting for you, for an interval, somewhere very near, just around the corner. All is well.
Henry Scott Holland

Every man desires to live long; but no man would be old.
Jonathan Swift

Old and young, we are all on our last cruise.
Robert Louis Stevenson, *Virginibus Puerisque*.

Life can only be understood backwards; but it must be lived forwards.
Sören Kierkegaard

Love and marriage
A man in love is incomplete until he has married. Then he's finished.
Zsa Zsa Gabor

Love is like quicksilver in the hand. Leave the fingers open and it stays. Clutch it, and it darts away.
Dorothy Parker

A happy marriage is a long conversation which always seems too short.
André Maurois, *Memories*.

Marriage is three parts love and seven parts forgiveness.
Langdon Mitchell

Marriage is a great institution – no family should be without it.
Bob Hope

Love does not consist in gazing at each other, but in looking outward in the same direction.
Antoine de Saint-Exupéry

Kissing don't last: cookery do!
George Meredith

Marriage is popular because it combines the maximum of temptation with the maximum of opportunity.
George Bernard Shaw, 'Maxims for Revolutionists'.

Face powder may catch a man, but it's baking powder that keeps him.
Anon

Wives are young men's mistresses, companions for middle age, and old men's nurses.
Francis Bacon

An ideal wife is any woman who has an ideal husband.
Booth Tarkington

A good husband should be deaf and a good wife blind.
French proverb

Love ceases to be a pleasure, when it ceases to be a secret.
Aphra Benn, *The Lover's Watch, Four O'Clock*.

Strange to say what delight we married people have to see these poor fools decoyed into our condition.
Samuel Pepys

The road to success is full of women pushing their husbands along.
Lord Thomas Dewar

Parents, children and families

Accidents will occur in the best-regulated families.
Charles Dickens, *David Copperfield*.

People who say they sleep like a baby usually don't have one.
Leo Burke

Parents are the very last people who ought to be allowed to have children.
H.E. Bell

I can trace my ancestry back to a protoplasmal primordial atomic globule. Consequently, my family pride is something inconceivable.
W.S. Gilbert, *The Mikado*.

The best way to give advice to your children is to find out what they want and advise them to do it.
Harry S. Truman

The first half of our life is ruined by our parents and the second half by our children.
Clarence Darrow

I love children. Especially when they cry – for then someone takes them away.
Nancy Mitford

Politics, politicians and power
Every country has the government it deserves.
Joseph de Maistre

Power is the ultimate aphrodisiac.
Henry Kissinger

Nothing appears more surprising to those who consider human affairs with a philosophical eye, than the ease with which the many are governed by the few.
David Hume, *First Principles of Government*.

A statesman is a politician who's been dead ten or fifteen years.
Harry S. Truman

Since a politician never believes what he says, he is always astonished when others do.
Charles de Gaulle

My people and I have come to an agreement which satisfies us both. They are to say what they please, and I am to do what I please.
Frederick the Great

An honest politician is one who, when he is bought, will stay bought.
Simon Cameron

Politics is perhaps the only profession for which no preparation is thought necessary.
Robert Louis Stevenson, *Familiar Studies of Men and Books*.

The ballot is stronger than the bullet.
Abraham Lincoln

The hand that rocks the cradle
Is the hand that rules the world.
William Ross Wallace, *John O' London's Treasure Trove*.

APPENDIX II

Religion
God is love, but get it in writing.
Gypsy Rose Lee

I am still an atheist, thank God.
Luis Buñuel

Time consecrates;
And what is grey with age becomes religion.
Friedrich von Schiller, *Die Piccolomini*.

If you talk to God you are praying; if God talks to you, you have schizophrenia.
Thomas Szasz, *The Second Sin*.

An atheist is a man who has no invisible means of support.
William Jennings Bryan

All colours will agree in the dark.
Francis Bacon

Faith may be defined briefly as an illogical belief in the occurrence of the improbable.
H.L. Mencken

Science
Where observation is concerned, chance favours only the prepared mind.
Louis Pasteur

Science is nothing but trained and organized common sense.
T.H. Huxley

When a distinguished but elderly scientist states that something is possible, he is almost certainly right. When he states that

something is impossible, he is very probably wrong. (Clarke's First Law.)
Arthur C. Clarke, *Profile of the Future*.

Our scientific power has outrun our spiritual power. We have guided missiles and misguided men.
Martin Luther King, *Strength to Love*.

The great tragedy of Science – the slaying of a beautiful hypothesis by an ugly fact.
Thomas Henry Huxley, 'Biogenesis and Abiogenesis'.

I almost think it is the ultimate destiny of science to exterminate the human race.
Thomas Love Peacock, *Gryll Grange*.

I don't believe in mathematics.
Albert Einstein

Speech-making
He speaks to me as if I were a public meeting.
Queen Victoria, of Gladstone

Brevity is the soul of wit.
William Shakespeare

An after-dinner speech should be like a lady's dress – long enough to cover the subject and short enough to be interesting.
R.A. Butler

A speech is like a love-affair. Any fool can start it, but to end it requires considerable skill.
Lord Mancroft

Speech is the small-change of silence.
George Meredith

APPENDIX II

Sport and leisure

... God never did make a more calm, quiet, innocent recreation than angling.
Izaak Walton

Fishing is always a form of madness but happily ... there is no cure.
Alexander Douglas Home

An excellent angler, and now with God.
Izaak Walton

Who loves a garden loves a greenhouse too.
William Cowper

If you would be happy for a week, take a wife; if you would be happy for a month, kill your pig: but if you would be happy all your life, plant a garden.
Chinese Proverb

What a man needs in gardening is a cast-iron back, with a hinge on it.
Charles Dudley Warner

People must not do things for fun. We are not here for fun. There is no reference to fun in any Act of Parliament.
Sir A.P. Herbert, *Uncommon Law*.

... I have always looked upon cricket as organized loafing.
William Temple

Always play fair, and think fair; and if you win don't crow about it; and if you lose don't fret.
Eden Phillpotts

Golf is a good walk spoiled.
Mark Twain

The English country gentleman galloping after a fox – the unspeakable in full pursuit of the uneatable.
Oscar Wilde

Travel, exploration and places
Very flat, Norfolk.
Sir Noël Coward, *Private Lives*.

Hell is a city much like London –
A populous and smoky city.
Percy Bysshe Shelley, *Peter Bell the Third*.

The English winter – ending in July to recommence in August.
George Gordon, Lord Byron

A journey of a thousand miles must begin with a single step.
Lao-tze, *Tao Te Ching*.

I have recently been all round the world and have formed a very poor opinion of it.
Sir Thomas Beecham

Polar exploration is at once the cleanest and most isolated way of having a bad time which has been devised.
Apsley Cherry-Garrard, *The Worst Journey in the World*.

Well, we knocked the bastard off.
Sir Edmund Hillary, after first ascent of Mt Everest.

America is God's Crucible, the great Melting-Pot where all the races of Europe are melting and re-forming!
Israel Zangwill, *The Melting Pot*.

The only way to be sure of catching a train is to miss the one before it.
G.K. Chesterton

They change their clime, but not their minds, who rush across the sea.
Horace, *Epistles*.

Whenever I prepare for a journey I prepare as though for death.
Katherine Mansfield, *Journal*.

Very nice sort of place, Oxford, I should think, for people who like that sort of place.
George Bernard Shaw, *Man and Superman*.

A man who has not seen Italy, is always conscious of an inferiority, from his not having seen what it is expected a man should see. The grand object of travelling is to see the shores of the Mediterranean.
Samuel Johnson, Boswell's *Life*.

For my part, I travel not to go anywhere, but to go. I travel for travel's sake. The great affair is to move.
Robert Louis Stevenson, *Travels with a Donkey*.

When a man is tired of London, he is tired of life; for there is in London all that life can afford.
Samuel Johnson, Boswell's *Life*.

Virtues and vices

A cigarette is the perfect type of a perfect pleasure. It is exquisite, and it leaves one unsatisfied. What more can one want?
Oscar Wilde, *Picture of Dorian Gray*.

A bore is a person who talks when you want him to listen.
Ambrose Pierce

A fanatic is one who can't change his mind and won't change the subject.
Winston Churchill

Fanaticism consists in redoubling your effort when you have forgotten your aim.
George Santayana, *The Life of Reason*.

Politeness is organized indifference.
Paul Valéry, *Tel Quel*.

War and peace
Sometime they'll give a war and nobody will come.
Carl Sandburg, 'The People, Yes'

War is nothing but the continuation of politics by other means.
Karl von Clausewitz, *On War*.

Since war begins in the minds of men, it is in the minds of men that the defences of peace must be constructed.
Constitution of UNESCO

There never was a good war, or a bad peace.
Benjamin Franklin

Riots are the language of the unheard.
Martin Luther King

The next war will be fought with atom bombs and the one after that with spears.
Harold Urey

As long as war is regarded as wicked, it will always have its fascination. When it is looked upon as vulgar, it will cease to be popular.
Oscar Wilde, *The Critic as Artist*.

Women and men
I expect that woman will be the last thing civilized by man.
George Meredith

APPENDIX II

A woman who thinks she is intelligent demands equal rights with men. A woman who *is* intelligent does not.
Colette

Man has his will; but woman has her way.
O.W. Holmes

All women become like their mothers. That is their tragedy. No man does. That's his.
Oscar Wilde, *The Importance of Being Earnest*.

Whatever women do they must do twice as well as men to be thought half as good. Luckily this is not difficult.
Charlotte Whitton

The male is a domestic animal which, if treated with firmness and kindness, can be trained to do most things.
Jilly Cooper

And a woman is only a woman but a cigar is a good Smoke.
Rudyard Kipling, 'The Betrothed'.

A man is as old as he's feeling,
A woman as old as she looks.
Mortimer Collins, 'The Unknown Quantity'.

I hate women because they always know where things are.
James Thurber

When women go wrong, men go right after them.
Mae West

Men play the game, women know the score.
Roger Woddis

Most women are not so young as they are painted.
Sir Max Beerbohm

She's the sort of woman who lives for others – you can tell the others by their hunted expression.
C.S. Lewis, *The Screwtape Letters*.

Work, business and money
In the United States doing good has come to be, like patriotism, a favourite device of persons with something to sell.
H.L. Mencken

Avarice, the spur of industry.
David Hume, 'Of Civil Liberty'.

There is always room at the top.
Daniel Webster

The trouble with the rat race is that even if you win, you're still a rat.
Lily Tomlin

Money is our madness, our vast collective madness.
D.H. Lawrence

If you have a job without aggravations, you don't have a job.
Malcolm S. Forbes

A silk suit, which cost me much money, and I pray God to make me able to pay for it.
Samuel Pepys

Work is the great cure of all maladies and miseries that ever beset mankind.
Thomas Carlyle

The almighty dollar is the only object of worship.
Philadelphia Public Ledger (1860).

APPENDIX II

The public be dammed! I'm working for my stockholders.
William H. Vanderbilt

It's a recession when your neighbour loses his job; it's a depression when you lose yours.
Harry S. Truman

Thou shalt not covet; but tradition
Approves all forms of competition.
Arthur Clough, 'The Latest Decalogue'.

Work is the curse of the drinking class.
Oscar Wilde

The superior man understands what is right; the inferior man understands what will sell.
Confucius

Money speaks sense in a language all nations understand.
Aphra Benn, *The Lucky Chance*.

INDEX

INDEX